T0171710

INDIGO WISDOM

Susan D. Topping

BALBOA.
PRESS
A DIVISION OF HAY HOUSE

Balboa Press books may be ordered through booksellers or by contacting:

Balboa Press
A Division of Hay House
1663 Liberty Drive
Bloomington, IN 47403
www.balboapress.com
1-(877) 407-4847

Cover art by John Mackie
Cover designed by Moreau Creative

ISBN: 978-1-4525-3220-2 (sc)
ISBN: 978-1-4525-3222-6 (hc)
ISBN: 978-1-4525-3221-9 (e)

Library of Congress Control Number: 2011920107

Printed in the United States of America
Balboa Press rev. date: 1/25/2011

This book is dedicated to my family:
To Don for his unwavering support.
To Nathaniel and Vanessa for sharing the good and the bad.
To Gib for teaching me the way.

Acknowledgement

While I appreciate every person who has shared this life with me, I wish to acknowledge my debt of gratitude to Barb, Mark and Danny for walking the toughest part of the road with us. I also appreciate the boundless love, acceptance, and support of my parents. They truly were the wind beneath my wings as I poured out my heart and soul for their counsel.

You must be the change you want to see in the world.
Mahatma Gandhi

Introduction

WISDOM LEARNED: Let go of the need to control.
Trust in the wisdom of a divine plan.

Outwardly, I am a confident, even-tempered, and good-humored citizen of the planet. It has always been important to me to make a difference in the world for having lived in it. I cheerfully talk to strangers in a store. I volunteer my time with nonprofit organizations. I try to leave people laughing. Yet inwardly, I am intensely private. Not too many people get into the inner circle of my being. That inner circle protects my quiet convictions, my love for others, my faith, and my soul.

When I began my career as a mother, with all of its ensuing challenges and concerns, my inner resolve was tested to its limits. When that happened, I strengthened beyond anything I thought possible. My inner circle grew past its constraints, merging with my boundaries and moving beyond.

I've been urged repeatedly to share my story because it is an interesting journey that might lend others confidence to struggle along their own paths. This isn't easy for me to do. I think I would rather run down the street buck-naked than reveal my personal life. Yet I would have loved knowing someone else trying to raise a spiritual child in an unspiritual world. While I was trying to help push a square peg through a round hole, I would have appreciated knowing it was OK to throw the darn game out, change the rules, up the stakes.

My definition of leadership is simply to step up to a task, something I've done repeatedly throughout my life. I feel courageous in sharing my story with others, but my purpose in writing this book is to demonstrate the baby steps I took to grow into an adult with body, mind, and soul better integrated.

I've changed the names of some of the people who shared my journey; they don't need to put themselves out there on this. I hope you will relate your own circumstances to my experience and grow to realize more potential for yourself as well. Have faith. Have courage to act in faith. Trust God. Trust in His guidance to expand your limits. Become more of who you are. Be in a relationship with our Creator.

When I assessed the confluence of coincidences, miracles, and grace within my story, I felt like my life had been given to me as a "connect the dots" picture puzzle. The dots, by themselves, seemed like chaos. By drawing lines to connect the dots and correlate one miracle with another, I was presented with a picture of the person I would become with God's supreme light shining through me.

I hope you will connect your dots to find a new you.

CHAPTER ONE

If you only look at what is, you might never attain what
could be.

Anonymous

Summer in Michigan is absolute bliss. The sunlight is intense, and
the vegetation is green and profuse. There's an abundance of water:
lakes, streams, ponds, and the Great Lakes. We live in an area that
values open space, so the activities of the wildlife are joyous to watch.
I'm thankful for every day.

One glorious afternoon in 2005, my dear friend Barb called
to announce an opportunity for travel. She'd been on the Web
site of Caroline Myss, the American mystic and intuitive medicine
advocate, and learned of a "Celebrate Your Life" conference to be
held in Arizona where Carolyn would be a keynote speaker.

When Barb checked the conference information, she was elated
with the caliber of speakers attending. The list was impressive: The
conference included Deepak Chopra, Wayne Dyer, Dr. Brian Weiss,
Doreen Virtue, and Gregg Braden.

"Feel like a field trip?" she asked.

"Yeah, I do," I replied. "Let me check with Don, though. He
has done more reading than I have, and I'm sure he'd like to attend
this, too. Besides, I have family in Arizona, and it has been way too
long since I've seen them."

My husband, Don, and I visited the Web site together. We had
so many miracles happening in our lives that we truly believed there

was something bigger going on in the world than just us. We were curious to see what others were experiencing. We decided it would be a wonderful vacation experience for us and quickly signed up, as did Barb and her husband, Mark.

The conference was wonderful. I half expected New Age goofies, but I was thunderstruck at how normal everyone was. They'd come from all over the world for this opportunity to learn and connect with like-minded people. The atmosphere was friendly, hopeful, and soothing. We loved every minute of our time.

I had signed up to hear a well-known angel therapist talk about angels. I had friends who were devotees, and I thought I would check this lady out for myself. I felt compelled to find a seat early and found myself in close proximity to the stage.

When the angel therapist took the stage, she walked the length of it and stopped and looked right at me. I wondered whether there was meaning in that, or whether I was imagining things. When she began her talk, I listened intently. I knew a few things about angels, but not much. She soon moved into sharing messages from the angels. We were all meditating and listening to her.

"Archangel Raphael is here," she said. "His message is for the woman who is in the audience today who has a book to publish and is procrastinating. She needs to finish the book, and detoxifying her body will establish a stronger connection to her guidance."

I quickly thought of the story I needed to write about my son Gib's illness and the lessons in faith that I learned. I had been told enough times that I needed to share that story, but I wasn't eager to share my private life with the public.

"This woman will know who she is by the gentle tap she will feel on her right shoulder at this time," she continued. I thought I felt three nudges on my right shoulder blade, and I looked sideways at the woman seated to my right. Her hands were resting on her lap. It's funny how a rational brain works. I assumed the nudges came from that woman. I immediately dismissed the sensation as my imagination at work. Afterward, I listened to another woman in the audience share her version of why she thought the message was for her. This led me to further dismiss my experience.

Further into the talk, the angel therapist asked whether anyone knew an Amber from the audience. Several people volunteered their Ambers, but she said no, her message was for my section of the audience. I reluctantly raised my hand. She asked how old my Amber was, and I told her.

"You're the one. Stand up, please. Someone bring this woman a microphone," she said. I was trembling, standing before hundreds of curious people. The message she gave me was from my deceased friend, Amber's mother. "Your friend knows you will always be there for her girl and thanks you for that." I was in tears.

"You have a special son," she continued.

"Yes I do," I offered. "He's a Blue Indigo Child, and he's been quite a gift."

"Yes he is. He has an important task ahead of him, and you are the perfect one to help him," she said. She looked at me as though she wanted to add something but decided this was too public a forum for the message. She moved on, and I was able to sink into my seat.

(Blue Indigo Children are youngsters believed to have distinctive psychological and spiritual attributes. More on that later.)

After the session Barb ran up to me, laughing. "I immediately thought of you when that angel therapist talked about the woman who was procrastinating about a book. You KNOW you're supposed to write that story. You're so busted."

"Not me! She was talking to that other lady," I insisted, although I did feel a bit shaken.

"What? She was talking to you, girlfriend. You know you've been told enough times to write it."

"Well, I've tried, and the words just won't come to me," I said. "Every time I try to go back to the illness years, I can't write. It's too painful to revisit."

"Yeah, I can relate to that," Barb said. "I've blocked it all, personally. There's no way I want to go back and relive that."

"Well, that's the problem with writing the book. I don't want to do it. It's done, it's over, and there's too much living going on right now to keep up with as it is. Besides, why do people need to know about us? We're not so interesting," I laughed.

I am publicly shy about being in front of people I don't know. We moved through the crowded lobby area of the conference center in search of our next session, but the book incident stayed with me.

After the conference ended, Don and I took a day and drove to Tuscon. As we drove, I kept having a random thought to visit the nearby San Xavier Mission. I dismissed the idea every time it occurred to me. I'd been there before, there wasn't much to see, and we didn't have much time. Still, the idea kept inserting itself whenever I was preoccupied.

Before returning to Phoenix, we had a few hours to sightsee and headed south to Tubac, an artist colony and rustic western town. I was driving because Don's driver's license was expired. As we tooled down the freeway, we talked about the conference and how much we experienced. When I saw the exit sign for San Xavier Mission, I impulsively exited.

"Where are we going?" Don asked.

"Well, apparently we're going to the mission church," I said in amazement as I took the exit.

"I thought there wasn't much there."

"There isn't."

"Do we have time for this?" Don inquired.

"I guess so. I just felt compelled to do this. We'll hurry. It shouldn't take long. It just felt right to stop here."

We parked in the dusty lot and walked toward the chapel located on the side of the church. The altar area was full of statuettes left by the faithful, and the cultural aspects intrigued me.

As I turned to leave, I noticed a niche with a simple stone statue of Mary. I thought, "Isn't that wonderful? They probably lacked the funds to have an elaborate statue carved." When the realization struck me that the statue appeared exactly like I saw her in my meditation, I stopped dead in my tracks and looked at her intently. How was this possible? What did this mean?

Don and I walked into the church. At the back were some paintings, and some of the subjects had auras painted around them.

I was struck by how the aura was captured with white light and a thin blue edge. It was exactly as I'd seen it around our son Gib. "Don, I'm having some major epiphanies right now. I don't know what to think of it," I whispered. Don didn't say a thing. A recording of Gregorian chants played in the sanctuary and other people sat on pews praying, so it wasn't an appropriate environment for conversation.

One side altar was dedicated to St. Francis. I'm sure the parish lacked funds for a stone carving. The parishioners put a monk's robe on a mannequin and laid it out over a coffin in the style of sculpture I'd seen so much of in Europe. We moved away to look at another side altar, but I felt an urge to return to the St. Francis area to pray. Don sat down and patiently waited while I ignored other visitors and prayed.

The minute I closed my eyes, I saw a priest standing in the foothills of the desert surrounded by Indians. He was European, and was frustrated that he couldn't communicate the magnitude of what this building needed to be. The natives did not relate to his vision for this church, and I felt his anger, tears, lack of confidence, and his sense of being so overwhelmed by this task. Every minute of every day, he fought his inclination to quit. Then I heard,

Is an hour of YOUR time so much to give?

I gulped. I recognized this voice. In my mind I thought, *No, I guess not.*

Then I saw a hand holding a pen, writing on a pad of paper. I was astounded, because I had tried to write on my computer when I'd attempted the story before. It had not occurred to me to write my story this way. Then I heard,

3:00

I didn't ask whether that was morning or afternoon, Eastern Standard Time or Pacific. The message was loud and clear, and I was going to set aside an hour of my time every single day until the message behind our story was conveyed via a book to those who needed to hear it. If I couldn't write in the afternoon, I would awaken in the middle of the night if I had to.

After all, it wasn't about what I wanted. It was God's purpose for me.

CHAPTER TWO

The dark moment the caterpillar calls the end, is the sun-
filled moment the butterfly calls the beginning.
Unknown

My childhood was that of a typical middle-class baby boomer: living
in a suburban home in a traditional family with a solid, parent-
driven core. Dad was a General Motors executive and he was a true
"company man." His work ethic was exemplary. He was loyal to
his corporation, a team player in management who loved being a
contributor to the building process. His work provided a traditional
family setting with a stay-at-home wife and five healthy children.
Mom was fun, affectionate, dedicated, and devoted to her family.
We were well-fed, well-clothed and well-loved. We were living the
American Dream.

After a day of hard playing a typical Saturday night was spent
bathing and then enjoying a bowl of popcorn while we laid on the
floor to watch "Lassie" on television. We knew we had an early
bedtime because Sunday school was first thing in the morning. Mom
always said they were laying a foundation. Sometime in our lives we
would need God, and we'd have to know where to find Him.

In later years Dad was a church deacon, Mom was president of
the women's council, and I was president of the youth group. All
three of us taught Sunday school at various times. Their work ethic
was rubbing off on me. Anything you wanted was obtainable if you

were willing to work hard enough. I set my standards high and set to work. It was all within my control.

My first bump in the road occurred after two years of studying fine arts at the college level. Mom and Dad committed to two years of tuition, but by the time I was to pay my own way, the first recession hit. They needed to concentrate on my brother now, and their support went to him. After all, they reasoned, "He will need to support a family some day."

I was devastated. I was forced to take time off to earn money by keypunching at a well-known local advertising agency. It was a blessing in disguise, since I met Don there; he was taking time off from his schooling to meet the same objective.

Don and I were the "kids" in the department, both of us eager to return to our respective institutions as soon as we'd made enough money. We were always together at office functions and soon became close friends. Friendship quickly blossomed into romance, but before we knew it, Don was returning to Missouri for school. Being separated was awful, but the semester ended with Don moving to Michigan to resume his job and start a future with me.

We married in 1973. We were quite the industrious couple, working full-time jobs and finishing our degrees in night school. We never saw each other between our hectic job and class schedules, and this was a time before cell phones. In fact, there was a major road where we passed each other traveling in opposite directions in transit to our schools. If we timed it right, we could drive in the inside lane and wave madly to each other before we were taillights in our rearview mirrors.

Weekends were spent working and studying. Don decided to pursue his master's degree in business administration full time by driving to the University of Michigan campus in Ann Arbor. In addition to working my full-time job, I picked up part-time employment to cover the missed income, since we'd just bought our first home. I was on the way to my first nervous breakdown. My father said, "Honey, if you two can make it through this, your marriage will stand up to anything." I wasn't comforted. I felt I was attending the "school of hard knocks."

The year I turned 28, after all this madness, I finally graduated as the only woman in my class at Lawrence Technological University with a Bachelors of Science degree in industrial management. Did I mention that this degree was accomplished during the women's rights movement? I was always on the front line, fighting for equal rights for the "Sisterhood." The U.S. Constitution declared equal rights for all citizens, and by God, I was tired of being told that I had to stay home or that my career choices were limited to teacher, nurse, or secretary. I was annoyed that a man needed to be responsible for my financial possibilities. I was not a raving feminist; I was assertive about my rights and abhorred "isms" such as sexism and racism.

While interviewing for a marketing manager position, I decided it would be irresponsible of me to take a job when we wanted to have a family. I knew it took two years of investing in a new employee before she started to pay off. I would not hurt a new employer and the "Sisterhood" by living down to what the established male management world expected of me. My interviewer was amazed by my honesty and thanked me profusely. "Oh well," I thought. "I will go back to work later." After all, I believed everything was within my control. If you wanted something badly enough, work for it.

It was a huge irony for me that it was so difficult to get pregnant. In our generation, we practiced abstinence to avoid getting pregnant. The birth control pill helped, but it wasn't infallible. An unwanted pregnancy could ruin a woman's life! Marrying under duress was often a recipe for disaster, abortions were illegal, putting your baby up for adoption could cause lifelong regrets, and birth control pills were expensive. Now I found out that I couldn't get pregnant. When did the rules change? I had believed that the minute I dropped my guard, I'd get nailed. All I can say is, if I'd known this, I could have had a lot more fun.

Don and I worked for this child. I took my temperature in the morning to detect ovulation. Don moaned when I demanded, "The time is now." I laughed that I'd remind him of his exhaustion someday. The humor was dimmed by the guilt I had for not wanting children in the first place. Who could blame me? I knew my life would never be the same. What about my dreams? What about my hard-earned education? What about me, the individual? Don had thought we'd be missing something if we didn't have a family. Since I was only one-half of this union, I thought it would be unfair of me to refuse. I knew for sure what I'd be missing.

I can't say that pregnancy "became" me. I retched for the first three months and wheezed for the last three. Fortunately, our first home was four doors down the street from my wonderful parents, and I could waddle on down to their house for amusement. Being the social butterfly that I was, I got along well with most of the neighbors. I was adjusting to being home, but when I looked in the mirror I was freaked at what I was beginning to "miss".

I'd spent the day with my mother and grandmother before starting my labor. It was a cold, snowy day, and I couldn't wait to return home to get horizontal on the sofa and finish the Valentine's Day candies Don had bought me. I thoroughly enjoyed my Godiva chocolate pig-out. Staying home was starting to feel pretty good. When my water broke, I guiltily thought I'd overdone it with that candy. I called the doctor, who said to get to the hospital in a few hours, and then proceeded to wait for Don to arrive home from the office.

I ended up with an induced labor, with all the hard work involved that you might imagine. All the silly Lamaze classes were for naught. Nothing happened as it was supposed to. Once the baby was ready, he easily slipped down the chute into waiting hands. I'll never forget him looking around, blinking his eyes and looking puzzled, as if to say, "What's this?" He just didn't cry. He was curious. I held him briefly before the staff whisked him away for processing. "Fenster," as we so lovingly nicknamed our baby in uterus, was sent to the nursery while I went to recovery.

By the time I was ensconced in my room, I felt like I'd run the marathon and placed first. Don and I gushed with enthusiasm.

"I can't believe he's here!" I said.

"Yeah, he's gorgeous," Daddy grinned.

"Man. That was something. Was I loud?"

"No, you were fine. You were great!"

"Liar. I made animal noises; I'm so embarrassed." We snickered to ourselves.

My roommate was sad with her circumstances, since she had an infection and was denied the joy of holding her baby. I really felt sorry for her, but nothing could dim my jubilation. Or so I thought.

The pediatrician peeked in and introduced herself. "I checked your baby and everything was fine," she said, "but by the time I was finishing my rounds I thought he was breathing a little too quickly. We did a chest X-ray, because I was suspicious, and discovered that he burst a lung. This sometimes happens when the baby is crying and gulps amniotic fluid during his descent into the birth canal.

You're lucky," she assured us. "A generation ago these babies would simply expire mysteriously. Not only can we help with this problem, this hospital has the only neonatal facility in the area so we don't have to waste precious time transporting him. We do need to admit him as a patient in his own right. Will you follow me, Dad? We'll have you sign the necessary paperwork." Don and the doctor promptly left the room.

I was absolutely blindsided. Not only that, I was restricted to my bed, unable to take control of the situation. I sat there, a frantic prisoner, while my roommate was gaily greeting her guests. I wanted to scream at them to quiet down, I was having a crisis. After a few hours, Don appeared at the door looking white as a ghost.

"Oh my God! Don! What happened?"

He slumped into a chair. "I can't believe it. I followed the doctor toward the neonatal nursery and found a couple of curtains parted just enough for me to watch the procedure. There was a team of people surrounding his tiny bed, working quickly. I couldn't believe it was happening. I just watched helplessly as this team of doctors performed a procedure called a pneumothorax. They pierced a hole into the chest wall to equalize the pressure that is causing the lung to collapse." Don looked like he'd been through a wringer.

"Can I see him? Can you take me there?" I begged.

"No, it's intensive care, and you have to wait an hour for a 10-minute visit. There is evidence of a strep infection, so he's on intravenous antibiotics to prevent pneumonia. They told me not to take you to the nursery while he's in critical care. If he lives through the night, his chances will greatly increase. Tonight is the determinant, and he needs rest."

We both sat there numbly looking at each other.

"Listen, babe. I need to go home while I can still drive. I've been up 48 hours straight and I'm crashing. I'll take you to the nursery in the morning."

So that was it, the end of our joyous day with Don shuffling out of the room with the weight of the world on his shoulders, our baby in critical care, and my performance as a birthing mother a dismal failure.

I tried to get some sleep. At one point I awoke to hear my roommate whispering on the telephone about how her roommate's baby "might not even make it through the night." I couldn't believe I was overhearing her telling my horror story. Mom had been right. There would be a time when I'd need God. I prayed really hard.

"Dearest God," I pleaded. "Please do what is best for this child."

Around midnight I decided that I needed to see what my son looked like. Don and I agreed that I could name him Donald Gibson Topping III, after Don and his father, but I couldn't believe our baby might die before getting a chance to wear such a wonderful name.

I dragged myself out of bed, held on to the intravenous pole, and headed down the hallway in search of the neonatal nursery. The attending nurse looked doubtful about letting me in, but I prevailed until she instructed me to scrub with disinfectant soap and don a gown. She then led me to his incubator.

Dear God. He looked so small and miserable. He labored so hard to breathe that his chest became concave after each breath. He had tubes and wires everywhere; in fact, he looked like a test monkey. I felt my legs start to buckle as I reached for a little hand.

"Sweetie, Momma's here," I whispered. He couldn't possibly hear me; his face was so distorted with apparent pain.

"Are you all right?" the nurse asked.

"He's in pain! Can't you give him something for relief?" I cried.

"Don't worry. Their nervous systems are too immature to register the pain," she tried to assure me. I knew what I was looking at. I was not convinced.

I returned to my room, supporting myself against the wall. Truthfully, I thought I might pass out from the shock. How could I have done such a bad job of giving birth that this baby was suffering so? Logically you know you're not at fault but let me tell you, emotionally you feel responsible for everything. I fell into my bed and cried into my pillow so my roommate wouldn't hear me.

"Lord, please let him live if he can be whole," I prayed fervently. "If you need to take him, I'll understand. Please ease his suffering."

It was a supreme comfort, after a childhood of rote religion, to have a belief system in place. I was in serious need of prayers and knew our families were with us.

I was awake all night, waiting for dawn so that I could call the nursery for an update.

"This is Mrs. Topping. Can you please tell me how my baby is?"

"He's just fine."

"Thank you." I smiled. Thank you, Lord.

The next few days were a trial because my delivery hadn't fallen within the parameters of a normal birth. The baby couldn't be held, I had to learn how to pump breast milk, and all around me were elated mothers exclaiming their joy. The day soon arrived for me to be discharged from the hospital and parted from my son.

"Please don't send me home without him," I pleaded with my doctor.

"These things are difficult, to be sure, but this is a pretty expensive hotel that your insurance company is not going to pay for," he said.

"At least let me hold him before I leave." I began to cry. Take my word for it; crying does not come easy for a control freak.

The next visit to the neonatal nursery, Gib was unwired from his monitors and placed in my arms. When I finally held him, I just cried. He was so tiny and helpless. I went home and mourned my empty arms. I missed the movement of him in my belly. Every day Don or my mother would drive me to the hospital to visit him.

One day, while visiting, I noticed him wiggling his right hand loose from the restraint. I was horrified to watch him struggle so much. The doctor in charge of the neonatal nursery was making rounds, so I called her over to join me in watching my baby as he freed his right hand, pulled his feeding tube from his mouth and grabbed the tube sewn into his left chest wall. As the doctor grabbed his arm, I said, "Now tell me his nervous system is too immature to know what's going on." I was shaking from being so upset. She just looked at him, deep in thought. I might also mention that in those days baby boys were not anesthetized during circumcision, either.

At last the day came for Gib's release. "Just take him home and love him," I was told. "Babies are resilient. Everything will be fine."

I snatched my baby bundle tight to my chest and fled the hospital before anything else could go wrong.

Homecoming was sweet, but briefly so. Our breastfeeding experience was also a nightmare. My visiting nurse contacted the La Leche League, an enthusiastically determined support group for nursing mothers, and even they gave up on us. Apparently Gib didn't have strong oral muscles for suction. I stubbornly pumped milk and bottle-fed him, determined he would have at least that advantage, but I was beginning to feel like the poster child for unsuccessful motherhood.

I tried hard not to be a nervous mother as the first year of Gib's life flew past. Gib was watchful of everything and could work up a good fit of fist shaking before he started to cry. We bumbled our way through parenting with our prototype model. Our son was impatient with us. He developed a method of communicating. Making a circle with his hand meant "clock." Sitting in front of the microwave meant "hungry." A humming noise meant "airplane." I was concerned that he wasn't using simple syllables to speak to us.

Pediatrician checkups were an insult as I continued to express my concerns that he looked jaundiced from time to time. By the time we got an appointment to visit the doctor, the symptoms had disappeared. She would look at me like I was a head case. I stubbornly pressed my issues. The fact that he was nonverbal was a huge concern for me.

"There, there, Mom. Just relax. He's just fine," the doctor would assure me. When I discovered that I was pregnant again, my patience with her condescending approach went out the window.

"Listen," I told the doctor, "I'm not hearing any baby talk and he's two years old. I should be hearing Mama, Dada, something. Unless you can assure me proof positive there was no oxygen deprivation, I want this kid checked out." After all, if I could assert my way through my equal rights experiences, I could certainly handle this mess.

"Well," she soothed, "You're pregnant and don't need the worry, so let's refer you to the speech therapy department at the hospital. They have a wonderful childhood aphasia center."

The speech evaluation was incredibly enlightening. The woman who tested Gibby was very direct and very professional as she described his aphasia. It was as if he'd had a stroke that only affected his speech. I immediately thought of his pneumothorax without anesthesia as a cause, but we were beyond that now. She said Gibby didn't even know he was supposed to talk, so therapy would be directed to achieving simple syllables for communication. Therapy would require two weekly visits and lots of homework.

"There will be many times throughout his scholastic career that you will be told he is mentally impaired," the evaluator cautioned, "but don't you believe it. Not for one minute. Traditional testing requires a verbal response, which he will always have problems with, but let me tell you," she continued, "This kid is NOT stupid. He has developed his own sign language to communicate with, and that is a sign of superior intelligence." Little did I know how I would cling to those words when the going got tough.

I drove many miles to therapy twice a week with my very pregnant body and my mute toddler in tow. We worked so hard to give him the idea of speech. Words were reduced to simple syllables such as "kiki" for cookie, "mama-o" for marshmellow, and "kaka" for cracker. When he'd finally utter a simple word for a treat, the therapist and I just about turned hand stands for the accomplishment. It was exhausting.

At last it was time for the new baby. The baby was turned in the wrong direction and the doctor wanted to use forceps to turn him. "No!", I insisted. Actually, "no" was about all I could muster in the heat of labor. The doctor was puzzled until Don explained our fears about another bad delivery. The doctor said I could try to push extra hard because sometimes the force would cause the baby to rotate against the pelvic bone. Trust me, I ran the marathon with that delivery. I broke blood vessels in my face, neck, and chest. In fact, I looked like a speckled trout according to the doctor. He was the cheerleader of the century cheering me on: "Look at that! The head is rotating! Push! Push, Mrs. Topping. This is terrific!" It was quite an experience. It was apparent to me that birthing was not my forte, so I resolved that two babies were enough for me.

We welcomed baby Nathaniel into the family with gusto. It was funny because I didn't have a girl name even picked out, I was that convinced we were having a brother. I was truly ecstatic. He gave me back my confidence. I could parent.

Raising the boys was like having twins, since Gibby's development was delayed from his rough beginnings. They ran neck and neck with their growth. I felt as though I had the puppet characters Bert and Ernie from "Sesame Street" under my care. Gib was skinny, cranky, and a worrier, while Nat was chubby, happy, and exuberant. They were everything to Don and me.

CHAPTER THREE

We must let go of the life we have planned, so as to accept
the one that is waiting for us.
Joseph Campbell

The first time God spoke to me I was sitting at my kitchen table
pondering what religion I was going to bring the kids up within. To
qualify for a dual wedding ceremony with our Lutheran minister
and a Catholic priest, I had to promise to raise our children Catholic.
Well sure, promise anything. I just wanted to get married.

Over the years I'd discovered Don's Catholicism was not
something he could renounce; it was a part of him culturally. As
an active Lutheran, I knew our religions were basically the same,
but I could not buy all of the rules and regulations. I always felt
Lutheranism was Catholicism without all the rituals. So here I was,
despairing to God about how to raise these children after making
a promise before Him to raise them Catholic. How was I supposed
to do that when I knew nothing about the religion? I was caught up
in trying to force my will on Don. Why couldn't he change? I was
home raising the kids, couldn't I at least stick to something I knew?
I was very annoyed with Don and the situation.

"Dearest Lord," I prayed. "How am I ever going to resolve
this?"

You are responsible for your own soul.

Huh? I about fell off my chair, my startle reflex was so great. I know that thought was loud and clear within my head, and I had not put it there. What the heck was happening? I thought a long time about that random thought. I know I didn't create it. Was I going mad? I gradually reasoned that I'd experienced divine guidance. As I mused about my dilemma, I realized that semantic issues were getting in the way. How could it matter to Him what method I used? Get in relationship with Him now, I thought. Well, if Don couldn't make the change, I would be the bigger person and do it. Besides, after a thunderbolt like that, I wasn't about to renege on that promise.

I was busy with the needs of a baby and a toddler, but I was concerned that things were not going so well with Gibby's development. I felt like he was losing his progress. Once the speech therapist said, "You know? I'm noticing problems with the use of his hands. Let's just consult an occupational therapist." Then a few weeks later I heard, "You know? Let's just get his musculature evaluated."

I was also attending a parenting class at the hospital to learn how to handle the overt physical behavior a speech-deficient child demonstrates. At least I knew not to accept a behavior at the onset if I didn't want to live with it for a long time. It helped to toughen my resolve as I firmly kept the picture of my end product in my mind. This boy would need to function within the real world.

By the time we started physical therapy, I was quite alarmed. Gib was so skinny, and he couldn't run to the swing set in the backyard without falling two or three times. He'd be sitting on the floor playing and he'd fall over backward for no apparent reason.

I remember taking him to speech therapy on one day in particular. My sister was in the hospital with asthma, and I was caring for her two-year-old daughter while her husband was at work. I waited with my niece and one-year-old Nathaniel while Gibby was being re-evaluated. After the evaluation, the well-intentioned therapist proceeded to announce the result of the IQ testing. According to her, Gibby's IQ was below normal, but I should not worry. He was capable of working repetitive tasks and living in a group home.

I felt the blood drain from my head.

"Are you all right?" she asked. "I'm sorry; I thought you could handle this. You always seem so strong."

"Well, not this time," I croaked.

I gathered up all of my toddlers and stumbled my way to the car. I remember fastening them in their seat belts, and I'm still not sure how I drove home, my vision was so blurred with tears. Once home, I had to work to control my emotions so my niece wouldn't confuse my crying with the fact that her mommy was in the hospital. I knelt in front of her.

"Sweetie, I'm crying because that mean lady hurt my feelings. Don't you worry about me; I'll be fine." She nodded her little head before she trounced out of the room to play with her cousins. I could scarcely wait for the day to end so that I could sob my heart out to Don from the safety of our bedroom.

"Don," I sobbed. "Something is really wrong with him. Sometimes he doesn't hear me, he's getting weaker. ..."

"Well he's NOT retarded, and if you believe that, you will limit him," Don stated simply. I wished that I didn't have to spend every waking moment of my day immersed in the problem so that I too could be relaxed about it.

I swung into a blowout pity party. I was commuting to the hospital twice a week with our babies for Gib's therapy, and one particular day I felt my depression really bearing down on me.

"Why me, God? What did I ever do to deserve this?" I sniffled as I stepped out of the shower. "I'm in such pain," I thought, as I dressed for the day.

The entire drive to the hospital I had my thoughts firmly focused on pity. I deposited Gibby with his therapist and then pushed Nat's stroller across the street to a pharmacy with a soda fountain. As we sipped our sodas, I overheard an older gentleman talking to the waitress about his battle with cancer. He was weak and could barely hold his head up. I thought, *Wow, he has probably led a full life, taking his health and strength for granted, and now he has to wage this battle.*

I looked at my watch and realized we needed to scurry back to the clinic for Gibby. While sitting in the waiting room, I watched a young couple with their birth-deformed infant. *Wow*, I thought again, *They didn't even get a chance at a normal life.* As we left the building for the parking lot, I watched a family struggling to get their teenage daughter's wheelchair through the door. As I held the door for them, the mother sadly looked at me and said their daughter was brain-damaged from a car accident. *Man*, I said to myself. *Their child was normal and healthy before being cut down in her prime.*

As I drove home I began to add up the math. *Oh, I get it, Lord. Why not me? I'm not anybody special. These people are struggling, too. It's just part of life. Live your best and maybe your gracefulness will be taken into account. Life is about what one learns from it.* I knew my prayer had been answered and I had been presented with an opportunity for learning.

The bad news just kept piling on, and I forged ahead. It wasn't an act of bravery; I just didn't have any choice. At the suggestion of the therapists, I enrolled Gibby in a special program through the school system. It was called POHI: Physically or Otherwise Health Impaired. It was a preschool program that incorporated speech, occupational, and physical therapy. Gibby needed all the help he could get.

For some mysterious reason that the doctors couldn't explain, he was getting weaker. His mouth slacked open, and he lacked the strength to articulate words. His hands were so weak he couldn't hold a utensil to feed himself, so I started to assist him. If the food didn't crest the back of his tongue, it would fall out again. The physical therapist rocked him in a tire swing with the fluorescent lights turned off just to calm his nervous system. Gibby was in constant motion and had to be physically restrained in his chair. He would scream his frustration to everyone. Sharing Gibby's world was a nightmare.

I will never forget his initial school psychological evaluation. The psychologist administering the exam asked open-ended questions like, "What color is this?" When he didn't respond, she marked the question with a failure and asked another. After watching this for a while, I'd had enough.

"Gibby. Which color is red?" I asked. He pointed to it right away. "Which color is blue?" He identified that as well.

"Stop that," she admonished. "You're invalidating my test results."

"So what are you really testing for, intelligence? I already told you he's diagnosed with aphasia. He can't reply to an open-ended question, but that doesn't mean he doesn't know the answer to it." I was exasperated.

I'll never forget that school psychologist. I'll call her Mrs. Smart. She had the ego and confidence of a seasoned professional, and no parent was going to sway her from her bullying tactics. One memorable conference that she facilitated was designed to bully me into putting Gibby on Ritalin and included the entire academic team, from the teacher all the way up to the administrator for the school. This was an eight-to-one ratio. I put a picture of Gib on the table before us so everyone involved would remember the child we were discussing.

"We recommend this child be put on Ritalin," Mrs. Smart announced. "He's disruptive, can't focus, and would clearly benefit from it."

"That's not going to happen," I answered.

"We insist. We are the professionals, and this child needs medical help."

"Listen. I'm his mother and I'm not about to give my three-year-old this medicine. If it interferes with his developing brain, I'm stuck with the consequences for this, not you. Besides, we don't know what's wrong with him," I insisted.

"Well, Mrs. Topping, sometimes we just don't know," offered another administrator.

"Well, guess what. That's not good enough for me. I'm going to keep looking until I find out what *is* wrong with him. Then we'll know what he needs," I responded tersely.

"In the meantime, this team recommends this student take Ritalin," Mrs. Smart persisted. I looked down the table at all the somber, straight faces staring at me.

I held the picture of our son before me. "I'm sorry, I can appreciate that you think you are doing what's best for this child's learning environment, but I will not drug my three-year-old son. I am not going to be left with a manic-depressive boy when he's 18 years old because we interfered with his developing brain."

"But. ..."

"I said no." I was firm. They all rose to their feet, frowning and whispering among themselves as they strode out of the room. I turned to Gibby's teacher, who was packing up her papers, and whispered, "Honestly, if this was your three-year-old son, would you put him on drugs?"

She looked up to be sure no one was watching, and then shook her head no.

"I'm sorry if this is inconvenient for you," I offered.

"It's okay; we'll manage," she whispered.

Gibby continued to weaken and I was despairing. I cried both aloud and silently. I prayed. I noticed that my joy was gone; it had been such a long time since I'd heard my own laughter.

The physical therapist eventually suggested a child neurologist to test for neuromuscular diseases. The day of that appointment was awful. I dropped Natty off with my mother and with absolute dread drove Gibby to his appointment. His electromyography exam — EMG — was another procedure requiring no anesthesia for pain, and this time I was forced to cooperate by restraining Gibby's head while his body was strapped to the table. The doctor then stuck large needles deep into the muscles to read the electrical responses to brain impulses.

Gibby's screaming was horrific. Sweat beads broke out on the doctor's forehead, so I knew he hated this task as much as we did. I held Gibby's head dutifully while tears streamed down my face as he cried bloody murder.

Finally, the procedure was finished and the restraints released. My son scrambled into my arms. Dear God, how could he possibly find comfort there after I was a participant? I could only guess the depth of emotional scarring.

The good news was that there was no neuromuscular disease. A trip to a genetic specialist also revealed nothing, so we now knew Gibby didn't have any of the usual problems. Autism was ruled out as well. Unfortunately, there weren't any answers yet.

About this time in our lives, my divorced friend Erika announced that she had a new boyfriend in her life. This was a significant event because it triggered a memory from our days of working together. I was just a newlywed when she talked me into attending a ladies party at a co-worker's house. There would be a psychic reading by a well-known local psychic, and although I was skeptical, the party sounded like fun. I hadn't been in the mood to share information about myself and thought the lady was full of baloney. In short, I couldn't believe I was wasting my hard-earned money on this.

The woman seemed to tell me a lot about my past, which I thought was a fishing expedition, but I remembered her saying there would be three children in my future. The first two were boys, close in ages and almost like twins. She couldn't see the third child, so she couldn't tell me much about that one except it was apart from the boys by a few years. The firstborn would have a handicap, nothing too serious, and although he wouldn't do well in school, he would eventually be all right. I dismissed her remarks because I wasn't convinced I was going to have children.

Now, as I stood before Erika all these years later, I suddenly remembered her sharing the psychic's prediction of a divorce from her current husband, and a relationship with a man named Glenn.

Wow, I thought. *I remember her saying the first child would eventually be fine. If that lady was right about Erika, she must have been right about me!* My hope soared for the first time.

Gibby's health was very bleak. It seemed like he was regressing in abilities. He screamed to communicate, he drooled incessantly, and he was weak. When I spoke to him, he couldn't hear me unless I grabbed his face between my hands and forced his face to be in front of mine. If we were in public without a stroller, he would lose stamina and I'd have to hoist him up to my shoulders to ride because he was too weak to hang on and ride piggyback.

I wrestled with my conscience to decide whether I should submit him to a CAT scan. I was bereft with grief. There was no explanation for this regression, and I just couldn't sit by without trying.

"Don, I have to know what is wrong," I told my husband. "It's not neuromuscular, it's not autism, and it's not genetic; what the hell is it? I think I need to request a CAT scan to see whether there is any brain damage, which I know sounds crazy because the doctors have assured us that couldn't possibly be the problem, but I don't know what else to do."

"No, don't do it," Don insisted.

"Why?"

"If it is brain damage, you will give up on him. Science tells us we only utilize 10 percent of our brain anyway, so if we keep trying he'll be forced to use some of the remaining 90 percent. I don't think knowing will help. We can't give up trying."

I knew Don was right, but I also knew I couldn't go on with this. Our boy was miserable. When I looked into his face, his blue eyes beseeched me. He silently cried out to my soul for help. I spent each and every day trying to find help and watching his teachers in frustration. I saw baby Nathaniel cowering, neighbors shaking their heads, strangers frowning, and pity on the faces of our family members. The people closest to me would say things like, "I don't know how you do it. I could never find the strength." What choice did I have? It wasn't like I could return this child to the kiddy-pound and pronounce it all a mistake. I was stuck in this, and it was more than I could bear.

The school's parent support group was helpful. We were all in varying degrees of family crisis. I was horrified to watch marriages split apart from the stress of ill children. Various do-gooder agencies would host parties for the children, and the school asked us to participate. That was tough duty. Our hosts would give us compassionate looks of pity and I'd want to scream, "I don't want your bloody sympathy. I want answers!" I would always return from these parties feeling like an old wrung-out dishrag.

I bonded especially well with Barb, one of the parents. Barb's adopted son Danny could talk but not walk. Gibby could walk but not talk. Together these two seemed to make a whole person. They were cute, in a heartbreaking way. We would get together for play dates while Barb and I shared stories. Our families were in crisis and we were living at the edge of a great abyss, watching our boys continue to fail under our care.

Barb had been down a grueling path seeking help for her son. After receiving his immunizations, Danny suffered seizures. The phenobarbital given to him for the seizures caused him to cease walking. A geneticist in Pennsylvania referred her to a doctor in Florida. That doctor tested Danny's hair and blood and found high mercury levels.

Barb was seeking help from a doctor of osteopathy and, as she spoke about treating the body holistically, I began to wonder about Gib's biochemistry. He had received antibiotic IVs at birth as well as treatment for frequent ear infections. Maybe his autoimmune system was affected. It was the only possibility that I hadn't explored, so I plunged into self-education. I became a frequent customer of the local health food store and read every book about health that crossed my path. One item that I'd learned concerned me tremendously. Sulfa drugs could cause liver problems, and sulfa drugs were part of Gib's medical history.

Gibby's school shared information with us about a doctor of clinical ecology that would be speaking in our area. I always attended every parenting class I could possibly find, since I found my parenting education to be shortchanged. It was a cruel twist of fate. My management degree wasn't too useful at the moment, and I was ill-prepared for motherhood. I should have been a nurse or a teacher; the establishment had been right! But wait, my work experience had provided confidence and assertiveness, and I valued these traits in spades. I would just continue learning what I needed to know when I needed to know it. If I could get through my work and college experiences, I could certainly manage the motherhood gig.

Don and I sat in the audience listening to Dr. Bugler, M.D., talk about compromised immune systems in children. Often this followed a heavy course of antibiotics. Apparently babies are born with yeast in their blood to offset the new bacteria they will be exposed to until the yeast and bacteria can come into balance. Antibiotics stall the development of good bacteria, giving the yeast dominance over the body flora and causing a condition known as Candida albicans.

After that condition takes hold, starches in the diet, when combined with the yeast, create a simple alcohol. The liver becomes overtaxed trying to filter all the toxins from the bloodstream, and the toxins become incorporated into the cell structure within the blood. The toxins that stay in the bloodstream carry themselves to cells throughout the body. Once in a cell, the toxin splits and divides when the cell splits and divides, until the body ends up with diseased areas.

Dr. Bugler talked about his history with traditional general medicine as an M.D., and his frustration with not being able to find a solution to help his own son's problems. Some research uncovered a school of thought within traditional medicine called clinical ecology, which treats the entire body for possible food, chemical, and airborne allergens.

These children struggle to thrive and are often characterized by being blond and thin, with very pale skin, "raccoon eyes," and red ears. If the immune system is overworked filtering yeast byproducts, it puts out histamines to fight imaginary invaders. The histamines make the blood acidic, which is what irritates tissues. Any tissue in the body could swell with an allergic reaction, including brain tissues. This could explain hyperactivity.

"Good heavens, Don, he's describing our son," I whispered.

Don nodded in agreement. "Yes, and we need to talk to the good doctor."

At the conclusion of his talk, we hightailed it to the podium to wait our turn to ask questions. At last, it was our turn, and to our horror the doctor was grabbing up his notes saying, "You'll have to excuse me. It's late and I haven't eaten dinner yet. I have a very long drive ahead of me."

"You'll have to excuse us, sir. You've just described our son to a tee, and we need to have you test him," Don asserted.

Dr. Bugler sighed with resignation and we were brief. There was no doubt in our minds that this information was crucial to us.

On the heels of that lecture, I called and booked a testing appointment for Gibby and myself. I was having dizziness, hives, and other odd symptoms myself, plus I was curious about the truth of this diagnostic approach. I started reading everything I could find about Candidiasis. I knew Gibby had been on antibiotic IVs the first two weeks of his life to stop a staph infection that had started in his lung. In my case I remembered an antibiotic treatment I'd taken in my 20s for an acne problem. Of course, our health insurance was not going to cover the testing. Thankfully, Don and I valued money as a tool to be used and forged ahead.

Our first appointment was grueling. It was a blind testing procedure in which a drop of an allergen is put under the tongue. The patient waits a few minutes and the symptoms, if any, are recorded. To reverse a reaction, a diluted amount of the allergen is introduced and the symptoms cleared. I don't know exactly how this works, it just does.

I watched Gib try to rearrange the furniture in the waiting room with a cane sugar reaction, cry incessantly with eggs, and go limp as a dishrag in my lap from formaldehyde. I was amazed. A four-year-old couldn't possibly fake these symptoms. He didn't understand what we were doing. When the doctor said, "Open wide," he complied.

My own symptoms were revealing for me. Pineapple made the veins inside my arms burn and soy caused my ears to ache, two puzzling symptoms that had been driving me crazy. I learned that bicarbonate of soda neutralized the acidity and could help stop the inflammations.

Once our allergens were identified, we could rotate our food groups. When exposed to an allergen, the body takes approximately four days to cleanse itself of the resulting histamine. That means that eating something wrong for you on consecutive days would worsen the symptoms until you experience a full-blown autoimmune reaction.

The food rotation diet required eating wheat one day, rice the next, corn on the third day and oat or barley on the fourth before you could reintroduce wheat. The same rotation applied to every food group. This diet brought us relief, and we were encouraged. I was diligent about avoiding processed foods, stuck to whole foods, and minimized our airborne allergens by being strict about household cleanliness.

I cannot be thankful enough for this knowledge. To this day, if my ears itch and I stop to examine my diet, I will find repeated abuse of soy products in my diet. If Don has a shrimp reaction and breaks out with excruciating hives, I can stop the reaction with a strong antihistamine followed by repeated use of bicarbonate of soda.

One time my mother and I were shopping in a department store while the boys played in the clothing racks. Suddenly Gibby started screaming and throwing himself around on the floor, as though he were having a temper tantrum. Other shoppers showed their displeasure, but of course I was used to ignoring the uninformed. I was in a quandary over the change in his character, until I thought, *Formaldehyde!* I knew it was used as a garment finisher. I scooped him up, ran to a drinking fountain, pulled out my collapsible cup, dropped in an Alka Seltzer, and he drank it readily. The tantrum ceased, but he was limp as a ragdoll. We left the store immediately.

It became easier to manage the screaming episodes as I resorted to the rotation diet, restricting exposure to chemicals and regularly having him drink bicarbonate of soda. I learned that formaldehyde was an organic compound used as a preservative for a lot of things, including pancake syrup and toothpaste. I was diligent about brushing his teeth with baking soda.

One winter we experienced a dreadful ice storm during New Year's Eve, and every member of our family took refuge in our home. We were the only ones left with power, and it was dreadfully cold weather. My parents, grandmother, sisters, and their families filtered in, bringing for the collective good all of whatever food items they had that might spoil. We spent the day cooking while watching the transformer in our backyard arc its blue light. We sent up prayers for that transformer not to fail. We had nowhere else to stay.

In the morning, as I wrestled with the breakfast problem, I decided to utilize an overabundance of eggs. Shortly after eating, Gibby proceeded to scream and pound the floor.

"What's wrong with him?" my sister demanded.

"It's an egg reaction," I realized and gathered him up to find bicarbonate of soda.

"Well, don't give him any!" she declared the obvious. Gib was hard on everyone involved sometimes. I can still see Natty covering his little ears to shut out the screams.

I thanked God for Nathaniel. That sweet little boy gave me my confidence as a parent. He was clever, affectionate, and seemed to be aware of trying to be the best boy he could possibly be under the circumstances. It hurt me to see him define a role for himself as a pleaser, so I chose to explain Gib's handicaps at a very early age. I knew he logically seemed too young to comprehend, but I intuited that some higher level of his knowing would understand that it wasn't his responsibility to make it better. Gibby was sick; we'd figure out a way to help him.

Nat was a teacher for his brother. Gib would see Nat walking backward and try to do it himself. When he couldn't, Gib would cry with frustration.

"Don't get mad at yourself. Try again," I'd encourage. An entire day set aside for certain accomplishments would often fall into disarray, as I'd be forced to reprioritize to maximize these little opportunities to learn. It's funny; we don't get to be the ones in control of life after all. What seems to count most is maximizing opportunities when they arise. I had become more flexible than I'd ever thought possible. Perhaps the measurement of success wasn't being in control but being flexible. It was extremely hard on everyone to have a difference in the family, but we were learning from it.

CHAPTER FOUR

The real voyage of discovery consists not in seeing new
landscapes, but in having new eyes.
Marcel Proust

One evening I attended a neighborhood Tupperware party. I thought
I might need a social diversion. Don was home early from work and
happy to see me leave for an evening of fun with the ladies. As I
listened to those gals talk about their children, my spirits sank. It
seemed that their lives were full of "firsts," and mine was full of
horrors. I returned home as fast as I could.

"Hey there," Don greeted me. "How was it?"

I burst into tears.

"What?" He jumped to my side to hug me. "What happened?"

"Everything and nothing," I cried. "They talk about toilet-
training problems with their two-year-olds, while ours is four and
I still can't get him trained. They talk about first words, and ours
can't even call me Mommy."

"Oh Babe, I thought it would be wonderful for you to get away
for awhile. I'm so sorry. It's made you feel worse," Don tried to
console me.

"My life sucks!" I cried and ran to our bedroom for another
heartbreak session. I cried myself to sleep, cried the next day, and
grieved to the core of my being. Eventually I thought to include
God in my misery. My heart ached for what Gib could be. No child
should ever have to suffer; it's the cruelest of life's realities.

Rationally, I knew this wasn't my fault, but emotionally I felt so guilty. If only I'd done a better job of birthing him. If only he hadn't needed the drugs. If only I could find an answer for this situation. Our child was an innocent victim. Mom always said He'd be there when I needed Him, so where the hell was He? I'd spent my whole life trying to be a good person, solve my own problems and make Him proud. What a waste of time. I should have whined and complained every step on this miserable path rather than waste my time trying to be a good.

"Please, Lord." I cried. "I need help. I can't do this anymore. I can't figure out what to do for him. Obviously, there's a reason he's here. He could have died at birth and didn't. What is the point of that, to stay and slowly fade away? I NEED HELP. I can't do this on my own. Please, if there's anywhere in this world that I should take him, then tell me. I don't expect a full-blown miracle. I'll do the work, but I don't know where to go next. Please." and I laid on my bedroom floor sobbing.

Of course, there was no thunderbolt. There was no answer, only silence.

"Well, shit. That figures. No one cares, and I'm in this alone." I eventually pulled myself together and left our bedroom to attend to my family.

Within three days I received a phone call from Barb. She had taken Danny to his holistic doctor and, while they were sitting in the waiting room, a beautifully attired woman told her that she knew of a doctor who could help Barb's little boy. This woman traveled to a doctor in Switzerland for a rejuvenating treatment that boosted the immune system. She went on to explain that the treatment used live cells from different parts of the immune system that, once injected into the body, sought out companion cells. The benefit of this was that it generated new, healthy cells to boost the body's immunity. The doctor was also known to help children for free.

"What do you think?" Barb asked. "Isn't that wild?"

Was this the answer to my prayers? "So, let's check it out," I said, tentatively.

"If you watch Danny for me, I'll go to the university medical library and research this treatment," she said. "Nothing ventured, nothing gained, as they say."

"Great." We scheduled a mutually agreeable time.

The serendipitous part of this news was that I'd previously heard about the treatment in Europe. I'd heard that the board chairman for one of the companies I used to work for, who was friends with celebrities in Hollywood, had sought medical treatment for youthful rejuvenation that used sheep cells. I'd thought it was quackery when I'd heard it, but there was no denying his youthful vim and vigor.

The most telling information came from a newspaper snippet I'd read within the last few months. I was an avid reader of periodicals. Motivated to stay current with the world while at home with children, I worked my way through two newspapers a day and several news magazines.

One day I noticed an article that said, "What would you say if you knew there was a treatment to wipe out most autoimmune diseases in the world? Such a treatment does exist." That was all that was typed, two little sentences. At the time I thought, *Wow. Wouldn't that just figure? I'll bet the drug companies would do their best to prevent that knowledge from reaching the public. They make a ton of money off autoimmune disorders.* I found it fascinating that I'd been prepped to recognize this possibility.

In the meantime, Barb had contacted the doctor in Switzerland. I'll call him Dr. Burke. He had lived in the United States for eight years studying under one of the pioneering doctors for the treatment before he returned to Europe. He was affiliated with the Louis Pasteur Laboratories and was a member of the World Health Organization.

The treatment was developed in a Swiss laboratory just after World War II and was a collaborative effort between French, English, American, and Swiss researchers. They sought a way to boost the body's immune system and found a method of using sheep cells that were configured closely with human cells. The serum was incubated in rabbits, much like smallpox vaccines. When humans were inoculated, the cells boosted human immunity until the body could produce healthier cell growth.

The doctor asked Barb to send our children's records to review and said he would call us back if he thought they were candidates for his treatment.

"It's a holistic treatment," he added. "The worst that could happen would be that the body would reject it and you would have traveled here for nothing."

Barb and I grappled with this new information. I was amazed at the possibility that God might have heard my prayers for help after all. I said I would take Gib anywhere in the world that could help him. I was thinking Switzerland qualified for that promise.

"Sue, what do you think?" Barb asked. "I'll continue with research on this, but I need to know if you're interested. I don't think we should be gullible. We need to really check this out."

"You know, I'm thinking this might be the answer to my prayer," I said. "I find it a huge coincidence that I've had hints of this in the past. Besides, if he's really with the Louis Pasteur Labs and a member of the World Health Organization, his credentials exceed anything we've currently had going on for us. Let's send our records and continue checking him out."

When Dr. Burke received our records and reviewed them, he called Barb to say, "Good news. I can help your situations. I will not charge you for the treatment, because the bad news is that you will need to come to Switzerland for extensive testing. I realize the costs are prohibitive for young families, so I have a foundation to allow for the medical expenses of children. This cause is closest to my heart, because we can make such a difference to the quality of their lives if we can help them early enough in their development. Every cell that is diseased splits and divides with the impurities embedded. With the cell growth explosion of a child, you can imagine how hopeless their chances are if not helped in time. Also, I must tell you that you will need to purchase human placenta extract at the price for which the laboratory sells it. The human placenta is like a megavitamin; it possesses all the known and unknown enzymes necessary to sustain life in the womb. I use it to maximize the treatment, and it is expensive. It is unfortunate that I cannot provide this for you. It will run about $1,000 per treatment."

Dr. Burke then went on to supply the contact information for an American patient of his who would help us make our travel arrangements.

"One more thing," he added. "I will need to see you three times at six-month intervals for treatment. It takes approximately six months for cells to rejuvenate. You must come to Switzerland the first time, since I have wonderful laboratories at my disposal. The subsequent visits may be made to a facility I use in the Bahamas. I try to close the distance as best I can."

Man, I'm in trouble now. Because Gibby continued to fail, I could never get it together to return to working. Where were we going to get the money for all of this?

One day, while at the kitchen sink washing dishes, I truly agonized about this dilemma.

"Okay, Lord," I mused, "I asked for the knowledge of where to take him for help, and this literally fell into my lap. I could never pass up the chance to help him, for I could never live with myself for condemning him to illness the rest of his life because I was a coward. But how are we to pay for this? We can't afford it," I pleaded.

You have assets.

What, assets? What assets? I mused. Where the heck did that answer come from? Once again I was forced to acknowledge the voice of guidance. The message provided began to enlighten me to the answer I sought. We had equity in our home. We could sell our cars, use that money, and lease vehicles. We could sell the 1957 Ford we had bought from my grandmother. This was brilliant. I would never have had the courage to think of that answer on my own.

"Don!" I cried, as I dried my hands and ran to the family room. "It just dawned on me how to afford Switzerland." and I laid out my revelation to him.

"I agree; let's do it," he said. "We could never live with ourselves if we didn't try. In my opinion, money is a tool to be used."

"But what about our financial security?" I worried.

"What about it? We're young; I'll just make more of it." I realized I couldn't love this man any more if I tried. Gib and I were so lucky to have this kind of support. Another mate would have left me for being a nut case. I also realized that my "revelation" hadn't just popped up; that solution had been provided for us. I thanked God heartily for his guidance and proceeded to call Dr. Burke for my own consultation before arranging travel plans.

Barb and I booked our flights and made our plans. We decided not to tell too many people about our treatment plans, because the news had been full of stories about parents taking their children to Mexico for a controversial cancer treatment. Some parents seeking Laetrile, a drug derived from peach pits, had their parental responsibility revoked by the courts. Since we were not too sure of our parental rights, we decided discretion was a better approach. All of our research indicated the body would simply reject this treatment if it didn't work. Dr. Burke's credentials were top drawer; he wasn't charging us money, so his motives were pure.

Besides, knowing as I did that this was the answer to my prayers, I didn't dare ignore this opportunity. I was afraid if I opened myself to help from God and chose to ignore it, I wouldn't be able to account for my actions to Him. I could just hear Him saying, "I gave you the opportunity to spare your son a lifetime of pain and suffering, and you simply ignored it?" Or worse yet, "You didn't believe Me?"

I struggled with my confidence in this decision. Gib was so weak. It was painful to watch him. Some days his legs barely supported him. He was like a newborn fawn with skinny, wobbly legs. When he fell, he laughed and scrambled to right himself again. One night during dinner, Don and I were haunted by one of Gib's neurological episodes. His pupils were dilated and his eyelids blinked in an exaggerated manner. His eyeballs jittered back and forth in his sockets. I wanted to cry. We watched him short-circuiting before our eyes. The experts told me to accept him for what he was, and I was supposed to accept this? He was getting worse and time was being wasted by inaction. If there was anything in the world that could help Gibby, we owed it to him to try.

Just prior to our trip, I watched a segment on television about satanic activity and possessions. The host was questioning a priest who mentioned heightened activity in Kentucky and Tennessee and in northern Italy and Switzerland. I had a sudden fear that I was traveling to a region of the world that was known to the church to have spiritual problems, and I was taking our son there. I was puzzled by this new information. I didn't understand why God would subject us to that. I spent a few days in deep thought about this matter before I decided that, since I'd asked God alone for guidance, I had to trust in Him more than fear Satan. Perhaps this was a trick to interfere with my relationship with God, to lure me back into fear. I put my trust in Him and went to Switzerland.

A friend of Barb's had a son who was at least five years older than Gibby and had a crazy, unexplained medical condition as well. When I met him, I was aghast at how he was an older version of Gibby with the same weaknesses. When he walked, his foot dropped and he seemed so unsteady, a wind might blow him over. Barb mentioned that a CAT scan had revealed what looked like pockmarks throughout his brain where toxins had deposited around the neurotransmitters. This child looked like he was headed for a wheelchair soon.

I was absolutely stunned by the similarities between this boy and Gibby and knew without a doubt that I was being shown my son's fate if I didn't act soon. Although I was terrified to leave the country for a doctor I hadn't met, for a controversial holistic treatment in a place where I didn't speak the language, I knew I would never be able to live with myself if I failed to act. I would be condemning Gibby to a physically handicapped future if I didn't try this option. Once I'd decided to consult Dr. Burke, I never looked back, but it was blind faith on my part.

March 30, 1985, was the day for departure. I cried to be leaving behind my baby Natty. We had never been apart, and it wrenched my heart to go. I grieved the entire flight, but once we landed in Geneva, we were ready to meet the doctor. We were exhausted with the jet lag. Barb navigated and I drove. The boys cried with misery in the back seat while we drove around in concentric circles trying to break out of the maze of one-way streets. When we found the hotel, Barb unloaded the boys and the luggage while I drove off to find a car park. I was convinced I'd never see them again as I followed directional arrows to a space well below the city.

To add to our stress, we needed to find food. This country had crazy eating schedules. Lunch ended at 2 p.m. and dinner began at 8 p.m., which did not accommodate the seven-hour time difference of our biological clocks. The language barrier was huge as we sought English-speaking people to assist us; all the while the boys fussed and screamed their displeasure.

When we were at last successful, I was appalled to watch Danny try to eat. He was even weaker than the last time I'd seen him. He used to talk to us, but now he could only manage to say, "Eat. Eat." Barb was beside herself with worry, so I stepped in to spoon-feed him. He was simply too weak to chew.

This act didn't concern me very much, since I had been spoon-feeding Gibby for a couple of years. The difficult part was the open stares of dismay, pity, and curiosity that we received. One young American asked me what language Gib was speaking. He was embarrassed when I told him Gibby was speaking English, and that he was speech-impaired. I was numb from the reality of our lives.

We drove to the town of Crans-Montana and checked into our hotel. It was a Sunday, and the church bells greeted us with a performance. Gibby laughed gleefully as he stood at the window, listening.

The following morning we found the clinic and had the pleasure of meeting Dr. Burke in person. The minute Gibby saw the doctor in his white coat, he started to cry. "What's this?" the doctor laughed. I explained Gib's fear of people in white coats; the people who poked and prodded him into pain always seemed to wear lab coats. Dr. Burke took his coat off right away and coaxed Gibby to him, and Gib proceeded to climb up into his lap and play with his stethoscope. As the doctor took blood samples, he told us about himself.

While at the Pasteur Labs, Dr. Burke had become interested in finding ways to cure birth defects in uterus. The doctors that developed the cell therapy treatment he employed received Nobel

Peace Prizes for their work. When the American doctor who helped to develop the therapy tried to make it available to patients in the U.S., he was told he needed Food and Drug Administration approval. Funding for that testing would take many millions of dollars. The government wouldn't fund it because it isn't in the business of medicine, and the drug companies weren't interested in something they didn't believe could be profitable.

"Don't get me wrong," Dr. Burke admonished. "I've lived in socialist countries and can tell you that socialism does not work. Except in medicine. There is no other way to look out for the peoples' interests otherwise. Wealthy Americans have been traveling to Europe to receive this treatment for years."

As I've already mentioned, Dr. Burke had moved to California to work under the American doctor for eight years while they perfected the use of human cells instead of sheep cells.

"We found there was less rejection using the human cell," Dr. Burke said. "In Switzerland, when a citizen dies, the state can harvest live cells right away. We have the highest standards for cell donation. The cells are incubated in rabbits to produce antibodies. The antibodies are extracted and centrifuged from the blood. The serum passes through 30 tests until approved by the government. When the serum enters the body, the different cell types seek out companion cells and generate healthy cell growth. We also use a method to extract toxins from the existing cells using ozone and nitrogen. Ozone excites cells and nitrogen extracts the toxins. It's quite easy. We affix a body bag just below the neck and introduce the gases."

"The third step," he continued, "is to give the patient extract from human placenta. Every known and unknown enzyme is present in placenta. If not, the fetus will spontaneously abort. In Europe, we harvest placentas for use in many health and beauty treatments. It is like a megavitamin for humans. I insist that my patients use this to maximize the effects of the treatment. Since this must be purchased from an outside source, you will have to pay for this at the laboratory's cost."

We concluded our initial visit and left for the day, knowing we'd have a consultation early the next day. We met so many ill people in the waiting room with wonderful stories to tell. They found that the treatment didn't reverse the effects of their autoimmune diseases, but it did halt the progression.

The next day we met with Dr. Burke again. While we were sitting in his office, he had to take a phone call from the U.S. Afterward he chuckled, "I'm sorry for the delay. That was a major American medical school calling about the possible uses of human placenta extract in treating children with cystic fibrosis. You will be hearing about a great 'breakthrough' in science when you return, but it's something we've been using for years." We felt humbled to be in on this exchange of information and did hear the announcement in the States when we returned home.

Dr. Burke went on to discuss his course of treatment for us. The test results revealed that Gibby's enzymes were out of balance and, as a result, his amino acid levels were depleted. He was unable to extract the proper nutrition from his food. Dr. Burke felt that the toxins remaining in his blood from his overtaxed liver were depositing in the linings around Gib's neurotransmitters, resulting in weakened impulses. I was able to understand this concept because of our experiences with clinical ecology and thankful to understand the concepts Dr. Burke was describing.

"You are in luck," the doctor declared. "We have just learned that the Japanese have had tremendous success using a species of shark cell in medical treatments because its cell configuration is quite similar to ours. We can use this to boost the amino acids. Amino acids are like a water barrel. If one amino acid is reduced, the others need to seek the same level, like a flood gap. The amino acids need to be in perfect balance with each other. The shark cells will boost the water barrel to full so that the body will know what it needs to do to achieve full ability. The treatment is expensive, but I have arranged for your son to receive it free of charge."

I couldn't believe what I was hearing. I had recently read an article in a news magazine about this exciting discovery and its uses for human health just before making this trip. I felt like I had been prepped for every eventuality.

The entire day we spent with treatments. Gib donned a large plastic bag and a technician pumped in ozone and nitrogen. Gibby smelled like the aftermath of a thunderstorm. We were exhausted after foraging for food at the end of the day, since the boys were not adventurous little eaters, and we went to bed early.

The next morning I ran a tub of water for Gibby's bath. As he played in the water with his little toys, I stepped into the bedroom to select his clothing for the day.

"Momma, I need this."

I continued fussing with the suitcases, rummaging for my outfit as well.

"Momma! I NEED this!"

Wait a minute. There was only Gib and myself in this room. Who was calling me? I poked my head into the bathroom.

"Did you say something, Gibby?"

He pointed to the handheld showerhead perched in its cradle at the height of my head and said, "I need that."

At first I was amazed that he understood how the showerhead worked, and then the realization dawned that he was speaking of his need, and that I was in communication with him for the first time. I was so used to weakened, unintelligible gibbering that I was overjoyed with this development.

When it was time to meet Barb, we joyfully greeted each other in the hallway between our rooms.

"Danny was walking a few steps this morning," she exclaimed.

"Really? Gibby was talking! I can't believe this."

As we drove to the clinic for the day, we heard the church bells peal again.

"Happy bells, Momma! Happy bells," Gibby cried.

"Wow! Listen to him." Barb laughed. We were truly amazed, heartened and humbled by these improvements.

We spent the entire week with treatments followed by some sightseeing. One day I decided I was up for driving to the Matterhorn to see its legendary beauty. Fortunately, Barb wasn't timid. The day was fraught with adventure as we found ourselves in a German canton, so not only was English useless, our simple French was useless as well. We guessed at the menu contents for lunch and laughed at the long names that meant nothing to us.

Sign language was required for travel directions, but we were appreciative of good-natured citizens who were willing to work with us. When the mountainous altitude flooded the carburetor of our car, I was thankful to know exactly what to do. Driving in the mountains required special knowledge for dealing with switchback roads, and I had experience in how to handle that, as well. I was soaring; I truly appreciated having the odd assortment of skills necessary to survive travel in that country.

Eventually we ascertained the need to park our car and take a train to Zermatt. Barb had a stroller for Danny, but I was forced to hoist Gibby onto my shoulders when his stamina gave out. As we walked through Zermatt toward the cable cars for the Matterhorn, I was getting bold stares at what I can only guess was my inappropriate behavior. I didn't care a whit. After all I had been through with this child, a few stares were nothing compared with dealing with my sick little boy.

We took the cable car to the top, and the boys were thrilled. Barb exclaimed, "We'll go to the top of the world to help our boys!" We were so thankful to be there.

On the train ride back to our car, Barb and I held the boys in our laps as they drooled and whined with fatigue. I will never forget the looks of sympathy we received and how they tore my heart open. One older woman just glanced from Gib's face to Danny's face. Her pity was written all over her face. When she looked up at me, she caught me staring back at her and glanced away. I wanted her to know that we were OK and didn't need any pity. We were foreigners in her country because we were in God's care.

CHAPTER FIVE

What things soever you desire when you pray, believe that you receive them and you shall have them.
Jesus

Our return to Michigan was wonderful, and the daddies were speechless with the boys' improvements. My father accompanied Don to the airport, and he was so moved that he could understand Gib for the first time ever. Gib latched his arms around his daddy's neck and wouldn't let go. I snuggled Natty next to me for the car ride home. He kept saying, "Did you miss me? I love you," over and over while I laughed and cried. When it was time to put him to bed, I lay next to him. His chubby little face was inches from mine with the biggest smile and bright, twinkling eyes. After a big sigh, he went to sleep. It was bliss to be home.

Shortly after our return, Gibby was the worst I'd ever seen him. He urinated on himself continually, couldn't speak well, kept falling when he walked, cried and screamed uncontrollably. We were in crisis as I felt all my hopes drain away. What was happening here? He did so well when we were in Switzerland. The treatment wasn't going to save us after all. One day, while Don was home, I sought refuge alone in our bedroom.

"My God, what have I done?" I sobbed. "Everyone else was right; I'm the one who's in the wrong. It's true; I can't accept him for what he is. And my stubborn willfulness has financially ruined us." I threw myself across my bed and wept my heart out. I felt all hope draining down and out of me, like a vessel with a leak. I will never forget how it felt to feel my spirit seep away. Soon I was spent, lying on that bed without an ounce of strength. When at last I dragged myself to the bathroom to splash water on my face, I thought *That's it, I'm finished with this madness. I need to accept him for what he is. I will never entertain false hope again.* I turned to leave the bathroom when I heard:

Don't you EVER give up on that child.

It took a full minute for me to realize what had just happened. Where the heck did that chastisement come from? I looked in the mirror to see whether I was any different than I felt. There I was, sporting red, puffy eyes and looking like a train wreck. Where did that thought come from? I knew I hadn't thought of it myself; I was in the depths of despair. I looked at myself in the mirror again, really looked hard. It was God. It had to be. I felt as though I'd been scolded. In amazement, I resolved that I would never again give up on Gibby, no matter how tough it was. When I left my bedroom to rejoin the family, I was a changed person. I had transitioned from believing in God to knowing Him.

Dr. Burke had instructed us to check in with him after a few weeks. I had to set my alarm for 3 a.m. to adjust for the time difference.

"How is my boy?" the doctor enthused with his deep German accent.

"Oh, Dr. Burke, I don't know. In some respects he's great; he's talking more and interacting with us. His teachers notice a big improvement, but in other respects he's never been worse. He cries constantly, is very weak. He wets himself continuously."

"That's good!" he interrupted with enthusiasm. "Those are classic symptoms of detoxifying. Give him plenty of rest and water. He will be fine. Don't worry."

I knew so little about holistic medicine then. I don't think I had ever heard of detoxifying before.

Shortly after our return, Mrs. Smart tested Gib's IQ again. She mentioned she'd run into my friend Diane at a conference and they'd had a great time discussing me.

"I heard about your trip to Switzerland," she whispered. Well, this certainly creeped me out. She was the last person I wanted to know about my personal business. I easily explained that I had kept my actions to myself because I didn't care to have Gib prejudged during the treatment period. When I called Diane later, she mentioned that Mrs. Smart had acted like she'd already known about our trip.

"Are you aware of the facts?" Diane asked. "Mrs. Smart said she doesn't understand your faith in Gib since he is borderline intelligent and neurologically damaged, and she'd had to struggle to get a decent IQ score out of him."

I was flabbergasted at this lack of professionalism. Why on earth would she be discussing our case with anybody?

Barb mentioned that Mrs. Smart had cornered her about the treatment as well, and had asked for literature.

"I'm sorry, Barb. My friend had a big mouth and wasn't someone I could trust after all. She felt Mrs. Smart was deceptive and led her on. She couldn't have picked a worse person to blab to, could she?" I grimaced as I thought about Mrs. Busybody.

"It's all right," Barb reassured me. "We didn't do anything wrong. The treatment is holistic and is available in Europe. The doctor has top drawer credentials, and we weren't charged for it."

As my mind opened and became sensitive to new modalities for coping, I came to grasp an appreciation for the psychic woman who so long ago had predicted the birth of our two sons. If she was right about Gibby's "handicap in school, nothing too serious," then she must also be correct about everything being all right eventually. My mother and sisters encouraged me to track her down and book a home party. I agreed, but was a little prejudiced due to misconceptions I owned regarding psychics. I'd heard so many opinions about the wisdom of consulting those people, but I certainly couldn't deny the help I'd received in this regard. Surely psychics owned a gift from God.

"Please Lord," I prayed fervently. "You've been with me every step of the way in finding help for Gibby. Please protect me and don't allow me to go astray." Once my prayer was given, I put faith in whatever would come my way. I found the psychic.

One morning I awoke hearing an old song from the '60s called "White Bird." I sat up in bed and I looked toward my dresser to see whether the radio was on. As I became conscious, the music died away and I saw there was no radio on that dresser. I was stunned by the experience. It took me several minutes to be able to get out of bed, the experience was so real, and the song haunted me the entire day.

By afternoon I was readying the kids for a quick trip to the store. I thought to call a friend to see if she'd be joining us for the psychic party.

"Oh, I don't think so," she said. "I talked it over with my husband, and he thinks it's the work of the devil."

"Really? Well, that's fine. I understand." I hung up the phone.

Hmm, I thought as I headed toward the garage with the kids. *How can anything that brings you closer to God be bad for you? And isn't it funny that she's more afraid of Satan than of reaching a closer relationship with the Lord. Fear really is our worst enemy.* I grabbed my purse, headed out the door, and thought, *Wow, I wonder if I thought of that myself or if God put it there for me.* I buckled the boys in their seatbelts, turned on the car, and backed out of the garage. Just as I put the car into drive I heard "White Bird" on the car radio.

I was stunned. I felt my heart expand. This was not a common song in the '80s. In fact, I hadn't heard it since my college years. I put the car in park, then sat and listened to the lyrics for the entire song.

"Thank you, Lord," I prayed, "for sharing my life and offering your guidance to me. I love you and will always try to live up to your expectations for me." I was truly grateful for this coincidence and was beginning to wonder just what a coincidence really was.

When the psychic party commenced, I shipped Don and the boys to my dad's house so that we could have a true girl's party. I set a card table and two chairs in my bedroom far removed from the partygoers where my cackling sisters and friends couldn't be heard and intrude on the readings. As each person returned from my bedroom to rejoin us, she'd share her stories.

Mom said, "There is going to be a new baby in the family!"

"I was told someone close to me would be pregnant and need my support," Lil offered upon her return.

My sisters reported, "Hey! Someone I know is pregnant." We all laughed about the continuity.

At last it was my turn to be read. As I entered the room, the lady looked at me and exclaimed, "It's you."

"What's me?"

"You're the one who's having the baby."

"Oh, no I'm not." I gulped.

"You have a problem with that?" she looked at me inquisitively.

"Yes, I do. This parenting thing isn't going so well for me. My firstborn has all these health problems, and I can barely eke out enough time for our other son. Birthing was fraught with problems. This is a dysfunctional household." I pleaded my case. "I'm not having any more children."

"Well, I'm sorry but I see you a year from now with a baby girl and perfectly over the moon about her." She sat back, almost scolding my attitude. I wasn't bothered. As far as I was concerned, there was no one on the planet who could sit in judgment of me.

"Not gonna happen," I resolved.

"She's a gift from God, and I suggest you accept her as such," she admonished.

I don't remember a thing about that reading; I was in such a shock. The ladies all squealed with laughter, but I just reaffirmed that I was finished with babies. I'd even given away all the baby paraphernalia.

–

The Michigan Metaphysical Society had a wonderful bookstore to peruse. I was a frequent customer during my self-education on psychic phenomena. A well-known psychic from Chicago would be giving readings, so I signed up. When the date finally came, I was excited because I hoped he could give me insight into Gib's problems. He looked at me in surprise and said, "You're psychic!"

"No, I'm not," I laughed.

"Yes you are, in an intuitive sense." He smiled. "I see you've figured out the universe."

"I'm working on it," I laughed.

"God's been talking to you, girl." He went on to describe my son and his issues, adding, "You know, there is a doctor who loves your son more than you do."

"How is that possible?" I asked.

"Because it is his purpose from God and he knows it. Also, there is a reward coming for the past anguish you've been through." He smiled and then continued. "It's not time to write that book yet; save it for the happy ending. Do not divert any energy from your son now when he needs you. Be patient. The purpose that you are looking for will come in God's time."

—

Gibby started school in the local public school system, with Mrs. T. as his special needs teacher. She had evaluated him last spring, and I'd spoken a long time about Gib's diagnosis. I began to share our problems with Candida albicans. Not only had she heard of it, she'd been under treatment for it for the past year and was horrified that he was given antibiotic IVs as a newborn. It was unusual to find anyone who believed in Candida, let alone a potential teacher. I took it as a divine sign and was thrilled at the prospect of sharing her time.

Gib loved being away from the physically handicapped children and with his new classmates who were mobile. Some of the children were hyperactive, but by now Gib was strengthening and calming down. I carefully followed the rotation diet, and, while some of his classmates ate Ding Dongs and drank Hi-C, my boy was eating almonds and fresh strawberries and avoiding bread.

I had been introduced to the concept of behavior modification for managing Gib's behavior when we were having speech therapy at the hospital, and I was relieved that Mrs. T. used this technique, too.

Gibby was very stubborn. I told the teacher I would offer her an incentive to use at her discretion. Since Gib was enamored with flying and with airplanes, I would take him to the local airport to watch planes as a reward. More than once I'd pick him up from school and the teacher would say, "Gibby earned a visit to the airport today." I'd alter my plans to accommodate the side trip because, after all, a deal is a deal.

Nat was attending preschool. Although he loved it, his behavior at home indicated stress. He was angry that I would be leaving him again to visit Dr. Burke. It's not comforting to think of hurting one child to help another. We shared a heartfelt talk at bedtime. I explained how I would leave Gibby home if Nat needed to see the doctor. Mommy and Daddy just wanted both of our boys to be healthy. He seemed to understand. A child's misconceptions could influence a lifetime, and putting one child's needs before the other's was risky.

Don was in Chicago on business, so I was flying solo again on the parenting gig. It was becoming second nature to discuss this with the Lord. Life was such a mystery. Why was I here? What was I supposed to be doing? I started focusing on what my purpose was in this life and asking why He couldn't just tell me.

Did your mother and father select your career for you?

There it was again: the random thought. The correlation made me giggle out loud.

"Oh my gosh," I exclaimed. "You really are the Father." I thanked him sincerely for the guidance, resolved to find my own path.

—

Danny was still at the old school, but Barb and I made extra efforts to get the boys together. Their roles were reversing. Gib was talking now, but Danny was so weak he could scarcely hold his head up. The treatment had worked for a while for Dan, so Barb was looking forward to revisiting the doctor at the Bahamas clinic. That fall we journeyed to Dr. Burke for a checkup, and Barb's parents accompanied us. The doctor was overjoyed to see us. When we walked into his office, Gib ran to hug him, crying, "I love you, Dr. Burke. You saved me!"

Dr. Burke had a visiting African doctor with him as well as the Bahamian doctor who owned the clinic.

"My boy! Look at my boy!" and Dr. Burke started to cry. As he wiped his eyes, he continued, "You'll have to excuse me, but at times like this I feel so close to God."

I was stunned. "Oh my gosh. I just visited a psychic, and what he said is happening."

"What did he say?" Dr. Burke asked, while the other doctors turned their attention to me.

"He said there was a doctor who would love my son more than I do because it is his purpose from God, and he knows it."

"He's right," Dr. Burke exclaimed. "I do love your son, and it is my purpose from God." We waited for him to gain composure and wipe the tears from his eyes before he told his story to us.

"You see, I was a doctor in Warsaw when Poland fell to the Nazis. Because I am an eighth Jewish, I was interred in a labor camp for the full eight years of the war. It was dreadfully hard work, and we were not treated well. I was in complete despair when I tried to kill myself by throwing myself under a moving boxcar. Fortunately, this attempt failed, but I was gravely injured. As the doctors sewed me back together, I remember hearing them say, "We need to save this one. He's a surgeon and we need him on the front.""

He paused to wipe his eyes again, and gathered Gib onto his lap.

"When I had revived, the Germans sent me to the front line to perform surgery on German soldiers. You can't imagine the horror and conflict in that. I hated these people; they had ruined so many lives. But I'd taken the Hippocratic oath, you see, and I was honor-bound to uphold it to save lives, even if it was detrimental to me."

I felt dreadful for him. I could see that he hadn't spoken of those feelings for a very long time.

"After the war, I was ruined for surgery. The smell of blood brought back my conflicted feelings about saving Nazis, and I began having anxiety issues. I decided to specialize in obstetrics. Do you know, the World Health Organization asked me to work in Africa? The tribes would summon me on their drums," he laughed. "My wife and I enjoyed our time in Africa. I became interested in ways to help babies with Down syndrome and had a theory that we might be able to treat the baby while in the uterus. My research led me to study with the American doctor who helped create the cell rejuvenation treatment. So when I have the chance to help a child like your son, I know why God saved me."

He looked so humbled, sitting there with Gibby on his lap. "Well, now," he said as he blew his nose and scooted Gib off. "Let's get to work, shall we? I'm a busy man! Just look at all the patients in the lobby waiting for my attention."

When it was Gib's and my turn for consultation, the doctor was effusive about the improvements. He gave Gib the serum, placenta extract, and the enzymes mucopolysaccharidase and optidase.

"There's something I'm doing that I need to share with you," I said. "I've discovered clinical ecology. It's a method of controlling allergens by rotating the food groups and limiting exposure to chemicals."

"But the treatment takes care of that; you don't need an allergist," he said.

"Yes, but while we wait for the course of treatment, wouldn't eliminating allergens help strengthen the rebuilding process?"

"Hm. You've given me something to think about," he mused, but I could tell he wasn't convinced.

The next morning we met our travel party in the hotel restaurant for breakfast. Against my better judgment, I let Gibby have pancakes for the second morning in a row. Within minutes he was crying and thrashing about in misery. Barb's dad looked uncomfortable in the presence of this mess. The entire restaurant looked our way and wanted my son to stop his fussing. Barb looked at me with a dawning realization.

"Sue! Formaldehyde! There's formaldehyde in the syrup."

"Rats, I forgot. I use pure syrup at home, and this is processed." I gathered him up to retreat to our room. "I'm going upstairs to start the Alka-Seltzer. See you in the lobby in time for the clinic," and we hustled off.

By the time we arrived at the clinic, Dr. Burke took one look and cried,

"What have you done to my boy? Yesterday he was fine. What is wrong?"

Gibby was limp in my arms, with swollen red eyes and red ears. He was disinterested in his surroundings.

"This is what I tried to explain to you yesterday," I said. "He's allergic to formaldehyde, which is used as a food preservative."

"You should have seen him an hour ago," Barb offered. "He was screaming bloody murder, writhing in agony in the restaurant."

"I gave him several bicarbonates of soda to stop the acidity of the histamines," I said.

"Hmm," he said as he studied Gib. I knew he'd be researching this possibility after we left, so I provided him with contact information for our allergist Dr. Bugler. I later learned that the two men contacted each other, and I was happy to have been a conduit.

The trip was fairly trying for Barb and me. She was overwhelmed with Danny's downward slide, and the news from the doctor was not good. He explained to her that Dan was deficient in an important enzyme that helps the body eliminate toxins. The treatment provided Dan with some relief, but it would never offer progress in healing. Barb was disappointed to the depth of her soul. I watched with guilt because we were being helped and Dan wasn't. It was one of life's cruelties. Danny was just as deserving as Gibby was.

One evening I watched the boys so that Barb could dine with her parents. I took the boys for a walk inside the resort and we sat poolside, watching people having fun and listening to music.

"We love you, Danny," I whispered in his ear. "We love you."

"We LOVE you, Danny!" Gib sang and danced in front of us. Danny couldn't muster a smile, he was so sick.

"Dearest God," I prayed. "He's just a little boy. Please help him."

An employee stopped next to us and said, "What is wrong with him?"

"The boys are here to see a doctor from Switzerland, but I don't think he can help Danny," I answered.

"I will pray for him." And he was on his way. I thought he was such a nice young man to take time for us.

Gib was tough to travel with this time. Whereas the first trip he was too weak and ill to muster a protest, this time he was letting me know exactly what he didn't like. On some level it was progress, I knew, but it didn't feel like it. I couldn't wait to return to Don and Natty.

Shortly after we returned home it was school conference time. This was not a pleasant experience for me, usually, and I was apprehensive about the true character of this new teacher. Gibby loved her. She was young, pretty, and no-nonsense in her approach. Dealing with a classroom of hyperactive children would require a definite talent for routine and control. I could tell she was puzzled by me during this meeting. Mrs. T. put down her pen, looked me squarely in the eye and said,

"You know, this is not the child I evaluated last spring. That child was almost too weak to handle the staircase for a second-floor classroom. This child has no problem. I'm usually not that far off on an evaluation, so I have to ask you. Did you do something?"

I gulped hard. I quickly assessed this situation because I wasn't sure about my parental rights. If I trashed my reputation by seeming foolhardy enough to take my kid out of the country for a medical treatment, I would forever have issues. Teaching staff would blow me off, doctors could refuse to treat him; I heard alarm bells going off all over the place. Yet her face was so open and honest, I felt badly for her. She understood Candida, so maybe she'd be receptive to our Swiss treatment. I decided to take her into my confidence and asked her for discretion. I was careful not to include anyone else in my story.

"I know I'm new to you, but I really am a rational, confident, careful person. I was the only female in my graduating class with a degree in industrial management from a technological college with only 3-percent female enrollment. I share this information to let you know I'm not an impulsive nut case. And I know full well what I'm sacrificing by telling you this story, but I hate to have you questioning your professional skills at our expense. Please respect our privacy and don't repeat this." Then I proceeded to give her a brief, abridged version of our treatment.

She sat back and regarded me. "Thank you for sharing this. I'm impressed with your fortitude; the treatment is obviously working. Don't worry; I will trust your privacy."

—

The Detroit Institute of Arts had just restored the beautiful Diego Rivera frescoes in its Rivera Court. Mom and I had studied art at the college level, so we dragged Dad, Don, and the boys for an outing to admire the restoration project.

While in the court, Gib kept breaking away from us and running into the gallery of 15th-century Italian art. I was thrilled with Gib's improved stamina and delighted with the normalcy of it all. After repeatedly chasing Gib and retrieving him, however, Don was out of patience.

"There is a huge crucifix hanging on the wall," he said in exasperation. "It looks like it's from a church or something. It is extremely large. He keeps standing at the base of this cross looking up at it. That is all he does. What's the matter with him? When I move him to join the rest of you, he just screams in protest. It's weird."

"I don't know. It obviously means something to him," I said. "Let's just move over to that gallery for a good look at it, and maybe he will be patient about letting us finish admiring this exhibit."

"He needs to listen to me," Don fumed. "He's stubborn, willful, and annoying. I'm really angry about this." He was tired of chasing Gib down.

"Babe, obviously it is important to him," I reasoned. I surprised myself when I offered another explanation. "You know, I'm sure Mary and Joseph were annoyed with Jesus when he insisted he be allowed to stay behind at the Temple. We can't possibly understand everything. Let's go have a good look at that crucifix."

The family moved into the Italian gallery. Gib stood at the base of that cross, just enthralled. That's all he did. He just stood

54

to his left while facing the cross, looking up at Christ with an awed expression. When we'd had enough waiting, we retrieved him to move on, but I felt sure he could stand there indefinitely. Mom said, "You know, I've been around a lot of children in my day, and I've never seen anything like this. This is very unusual."

"I know, Mom. I wonder why it means so much to him." All of us considered this experience a little unnerving.

CHAPTER SIX

To one who has faith, no explanation is necessary. To one
without faith, no explanation is possible.
St. Thomas Aquinas

My psychic party experiences caused me to be more open-minded
to the metaphysical. I noticed our son had a knack for reading my
mind. God had been sending me random thoughts. Surely there was
more to life than what was conventionally believed. Otherwise, what
could explain the wonderful events happening in our lives?

I was a regular at the local health food store and Cheryl, the
owner, happened to say to me one day, "You know, I have a friend
who will teach psychic awareness. I'm thinking of offering classes in
my store after hours. Would you be interested?"

There was no denying to myself that I was on a knowledge quest
in this regard, and I hated being ignorant on a subject. I also prefer to
form my own opinion on topics, and you can't have an opinion if you
haven't studied both sides of an issue. I agreed to join the classes.

Elaine taught the class, and she was awesome. Imagine my
surprise when Mrs. T. showed up for class. What a coincidence,
I thought. Elaine taught us how to meditate, how to see auras,
and how to listen to intuition. I must admit that I wasn't very
successful, but I did enjoy meditation. I'd heard a priest interviewed
on television say that prayer was our talking to God, meditation
was Him answering. Elaine explained that our souls could go "out
of body" in the astral plane, and that a soul could choose any age

within its lifetime to appear to us. She talked about reincarnation as well as earthbound spirits.

None of this frightened me, but I sure didn't know what the heck she was talking about. Thus I began my education. I read everything: Edgar Cayce, Ruth Montgomery, "The Tibetan Book of the Dead," the Bible, and books about all religions. I found my way to the doorstep of a metaphysical bookstore. The bookstore featured mediums from time to time, and although I couldn't afford to sign up for very much, I did manage a reading with Mrs. Fall, a woman from England who channeled guidance from the other side. I was open to learning about the crazy things I'd never heard of before. I prayed to God my usual prayer of protection and guidance, and then I proceeded with full confidence that my prayer would be answered.

I really believe that we don't need to consult psychic readers for guidance in our daily lives. We're put on this earth to learn something during our time here. The lessons come from the searching.

I know that the Bible's position on this subject is to avoid soothsayers and astrologers, and I couldn't agree more. There are some real creeps out there. It is spiritually risky to not be careful. Yet I also don't believe for one minute that God quit talking to us, or quit sending us guidance, after the Bible was written. I've always felt He had a hand in what our talents would be; it's up to us to use those gifts responsibly. We had a son with spiritual gifts, and it was our responsibility to guide him. I knew God was answering my prayers, so if I prayed for guidance and protection, I had faith. Certain doors opened, and I walked through in trust.

When I saw Mrs. Fall, I was intrigued. She looked over my left shoulder the entire time and just talked away while the tape recorder captured her comments. She delivered messages from my mother's father, whom I never knew, and described his gestures and mannerisms as he spoke to her. Always the skeptic, I returned home and called my grandmother.

"Guess who I was talking with today?"

"Who?" she asked.

"Grandpa! Oscar, you know, your husband." I continued with the details and she affirmed everything with delight. I was reassured with my course of action. I wasn't seeking the psychics. They were opportunities put before me from which to learn. I remembered clearly the time God had told me I was responsible for my own soul. Since I took that responsibility, my intuition had become my guidance and protection. My relationship with God was becoming stronger with each experience, and I grew to understand Him as my life force.

—

The fall conference at Gib's school was interesting. The new speech therapist introduced herself and said she'd been through the records from the POHI program as well as the hospital. The reports covered his behavior disorders, echolalia (repetitive vocalizations), perseveration behavior (repetitive actions), and hyperactivity, yet she saw no evidence of this.

"How does phenomenal change like this happen in such a short period?" she asked. "This is outstanding."

"Well, sit back." I laughed, and proceeded to share our story. The director entered as I finished, and it was as though his ego couldn't help surfacing.

"The important thing is for you to accept this child for what he is," he pronounced. I was dumbfounded. How many times had I been callously told this? Was this standard training for these people?

"Just what IS my child? Please tell me, because no one else has ever told me what he is," I said.

"Well, they may not know," he tossed out.

I said, "Guess what? That's not good enough for me. If I'd 'accepted him' for what he appeared to be and not gone to Switzerland for treatment, we'd not have experienced a fraction of the improvements we've seen in him over the last six months."

"What treatment?" Everyone laughed and assured him they'd fill him in later. Honestly, how many less assertive parents had been shot out of the realm of hopefulness by misguided professionals like this man?

During this period I was being extra careful about the pending pregnancy that had been foretold. The clues just kept dropping in. While working the crossword puzzle in the newspaper, I'd randomly glance at my horoscope. I didn't have any use for the horoscope; it was just there. "Don't deny the inevitable," it would say. Or, "Accept your gift from God." I'd laugh about coincidences, and my friend Lil would find them entertaining.

"Well, you know," she said quite simply, "if it's what the Lord intends, I don't think you want to ignore Him."

She was right, of course. He'd been with me in bad times; maybe I was destined to get a break here. I took it to prayer.

"OK, Lord," I prayed. "If this baby is something I must do, I'll accept it. But I need a healthy child because I'm quite maxed out."

Don had developed shingles from all the stress that constituted our life, as we knew it then. It was quite obvious I could not return to the work force, so he threw himself into being the best provider he could possibly be. Like I said, it wasn't easy having this difference in the family. He'd changed employers, his responsibilities had increased, and he'd been forced to trust my judgment in regard to Gib. We'd refinanced our home. It wasn't surprising that he'd contracted one huge autoimmune response. He was livid with a rash that crept around his belly and down his arms. He'd feel on fire with what he took to calling "fraz attacks." He'd be in a meeting at work when the "fraz" would start. He'd run down the hall toward the sanctuary of his office in complete agony, with one arm flailing about.

I felt awful for him. In fact, we couldn't share a bed because bumping against him could trigger another burning attack. His doctor remarked that he'd never seen such a severe case of shingles in anyone so young.

While I was sleeping in the guest room during this period, I'd developed a lingering flu bug. I'd been so sick; my menstrual cycle had been delayed. I called my doctor for a checkup to make sure there wasn't something severely wrong with me.

"Any chance that you're pregnant?" the nurse asked.

"Gosh, I suppose so. I'm not on the pill or anything, but I don't see how I could be. My husband has the shingles." I half giggled. It was embarrassing to be offering up this much information.

The office ran the tests, and when they called to tell me I was pregnant, I burst out crying. I was so stunned; I sat down abruptly, right where I was standing.

"I'm sorry; is this a problem?" the nurse inquired.

"I just thought I had the flu!" I cried. How stupid I sounded; how many years had I been married?

"Are you alone? Should I call someone for you?" What must she be thinking, I wondered.

"No," I sniffed. "It's not a big problem; it's just that I'm overwhelmed." I sat by the phone for a long time before calling Don.

"Hi, Hon," I started, innocently enough.

"What's up?" he asked, simply because I rarely bothered him at work.

"You know that flu bug? Well, the doctor just called to tell me we're pregnant."

"WHAT?"

"I'm pregnant."

"Well, how the hell did that happen?"

"I don't know, Don. In the usual way, I guess."

"Was I there? We haven't been sleeping together, so how did the sperm even get there?" he asked. I laughed because I couldn't tell whether he was serious or not.

"Well, we must have done something!"

"Wouldn't we remember that? What is this, the immaculate conception?" he joked feebly.

"Don't be ridiculous."

"That psychic lady probably put a hex on our bed," Don scoffed.

"Stop." I wondered how this went in other families.

"Well, all I know is, this kid better have blue eyes," he half teased.

My family and friends were amused and took to calling the baby heavenly names, like Celeste. I complained to anyone who would listen. I was supposed to be calling the shots here, and I'd forgotten I'd given my permission to accept this gift. All I knew was that I could barely handle the two we had, so I really believed a third child would put me over the edge.

Our third trip to Dr. Burke was approaching fast, and I decided we had to purchase the treatment for Don. I now realized shingles were caused by a weakened immune system that could no longer control the chickenpox virus that still resided in Don's body. I really had to convince him to spend the money on himself.

"Sweetie, you are our only provider. We can't afford for you to have health issues, too. We must boost your immune system," I reasoned.

Don agreed; he felt so lousy with these outbreaks. We booked our trip and prepared for a family adventure.

Being pregnant and traveling through Europe was exhausting. The third pregnancy really pooched my stomach out sooner than it should have. The boys were 3 and 5 years old and not inclined toward enjoying non-American cuisine, so we'd strike a bargain.

"If we take you to Burger King, then you must sit with us at our meal in a nice restaurant," we told them. They'd agree, and it was embarrassing to watch them eat jumbo-sized portions, as if they'd never seen real food before. We must have looked like poster children for American bad eating habits. Also, traveling with tykes required frequent trips to restrooms, which could only be found in train stations.

Don and Gib received their treatments daily, and we loved April in Switzerland. The boys loved to hear snow guns doing avalanche control and squealed when they heard the "happy bells" of the churches. Easter found us dining in our hotel, enjoying a fondue dinner, and watching a beautiful snow falling outside. We saw many rainbows, and Gib took to calling them "God smiles."

When clinic was over, Dr. Burke invited us to his home in Lugano, just north of the Italian border. We followed Dr. and Mrs. Burke to the top of the Alps. It was a barren, windswept place, and the altitude caused our car to stall. We watched helplessly as the doctor's car disappeared over the horizon, and there was no way to stop him.

Don tried to start the engine. "Now, what? There's nothing around. We're in the middle of nowhere," he fussed.

"Just a minute," I said and quickly said a prayer asking God to intervene. After I finished, I said, "Okay, try it again."

The engine roared to life. Don just looked at me. "How did you know the engine would start?"

"Honestly, just ask and ye shall receive," I smirked. "That's what this whole treatment thing is about, you know."

We sped off to catch up to the doctor. Don kept glancing at me warily while I smiled and looked out the window. I silently thanked God for his help.

We soon found a train station for a bathroom break. Don took Gibby with him, and Natty went along with me. We entered a stall, and I locked the door behind us. Unfortunately, I couldn't figure out the locking mechanism to get the door open. There wasn't enough of a crawl space above or below the door for us to escape, so I kept pestering the lock. I heard someone enter the restroom, so I said, "Excuse me, could you please help us? We're locked in here."

No answer.

"Hello? Could you help me? We're locked in."

I heard the water in the sink turn on and off, then a quick exit.

Great. "HELP!" I started to yell. "Somebody, please help!" My poor toddler covered his ears with his hands.

"I'm sorry, sweetie. HELP! Someone has to hear us. HELP!" Natty started to whimper. Surely Don would wonder where we were and come looking for us.

"HELP!" Where the heck was Don?

Damn. By now I was throwing brute strength into that lock. Click. It opened with suspicious ease, as though nothing had been wrong with it in the first place. Natty and I fell out of the stall, totally flustered. After washing our hands, we hastily tumbled out of the restroom past a very distraught looking woman in the hallway.

She must have been standing out there listening to us, wondering what we were saying. It seemed to me common sense would prompt you to get the authorities. Wouldn't yelling be a clue that something was wrong?

I later laughed to myself, wondering what the lady thought. I had probably fed someone's preconceived ideas about inappropriate American behavior. For the time being, I was a woman with a mission, and that was to reunite with my husband.

There he was, standing in the parking lot and shooting the breeze with Dr. Burke. "What took you so long?" he asked. I resisted the urge to kill him in front of the doctor.

"Trapped in a toilet stall. Didn't you wonder if you should look for us?" Nat scampered into the backseat of our car, and he wasn't going to budge from that spot. His eyes were huge, as if he'd been in the company of madness.

"A toilet stall!" both Don and Dr. Burke started laughing. "How did that happen?"

"I couldn't get the locking mechanism to work. Quit laughing. I'm not laughing. I'm seriously traumatized."

We all piled into our respective vehicles and finished the drive to Lugano, but Nat never recovered from that experience. For the rest of the trip, he refused to accompany me into a restroom.

Lugano was a pleasant surprise. The climate was unusual. We felt like we were in the mountains, but Lugano was at sea level and there were palm trees growing. The Italian influence was everywhere. While trying to find a car park, a gendarme was speaking Italian to us, and we were unable to communicate. Don had studied Latin in high school, so he could understand her well enough but was unable to respond. Fortunately, she understood French so between the three of us there was some communication.

Ordering lunch meat at a market was hysterical, as neither English nor French was useful, and the clerks started yelling their questions, as though volume would make the difference. We eventually resorted to grunts and sign language, with a lot of laughter. It was riotous.

Dr. and Mrs. Burke had invited us to their home for dinner, and they were delightful hosts. They were affectionate with the boys, and Dr. Burke chided me for my attitude about the pregnancy.

"You know," he admonished, "there has been a lot of research to prove that infants are sensitive to their mother's attitudes and language while in the uterus. I suggest you make up your mind to be in favor of this child and watch what you say." Just that simple rebuke caused me to change my attitude and be appreciative of this gift.

The next day, while sightseeing with the boys, we dropped by a 15th-century Italianate church. We were amazed at the differences between this building and the churches we had seen elsewhere in Europe. There weren't any pews to sit on; the masses of people had to stand.

Gibby broke away from us and made a beeline to the altar, where he stood looking up at a huge crucifix. I was reminded of the afternoon in the Detroit Institute of Arts. I encouraged Don to let him stay there, since he wasn't bothering anything or anyone. We had the church to ourselves. Don, Natty, and I took our time inspecting the side altar areas. Near the door was a really large glass case full of dolls attired in religious costumes that depicted different Biblical stories. We spent quite a while telling some of the stories to Nat while Gib remained by the crucifix.

As we prepared to leave, Don said, "I'll retrieve Gibby and meet you in front of the church."

"OK," I agreed and grabbed Natty's little hand. We turned toward the door and just before we exited, I noticed a brass plaque with a slit in it that was eye level to me. The plaque said something in Latin or Italian; I didn't understand why it was there or its purpose.

A few minutes later, Don burst out the front door and came to the sidewalk where we were waiting.

"Do you have any money?" he asked.

"Yeah."

"Give me some, OK?"

"All right. What's up?" I asked, as I fished around in my wallet.

"I'll tell you about it in a minute." He dashed back inside the church.

In a few moments Don reappeared with Gibby in tow. The boys grabbed hands and walked in front of us. Gosh, they could be so cute sometimes.

"Do you want to tell me what that was about?" I murmured.

"Did you notice a brass plaque as you were leaving?" I nodded my head. "Just as we started to open the door, Gib said, 'Wait, Dad. You've got to put money in that for the dolls.' That plaque was nowhere near those dolls, and it was eye level to me, so how did he even see it? When I stopped to look at the plaque, it said, 'Contributions for Religious Dolls' in Latin. How the hell did he know that?" Don sputtered.

"I keep telling you, he's not your average kid," I laughed.

Don was silent for several minutes as we walked away from the church.

CHAPTER SEVEN

It is time to trust that small voice within, coming from
the person we really are. It is time to look within and to
uncover all that has been blocking us from our truth.

Unknown

I was so grateful for God's guidance. Gib was nearly normal now.
His screaming was replaced by laughter, and he could talk to us.
He could tell us where he hurt, ask a question, talk back to us.
He and his brother could interact. Not only could he feed himself
with gusto, he could also write his name and a few other words.
The drooling and slack jaw were replaced by smiles. His kisses were
wonderful. He had never had enough strength for oral control, and
now I caught him trying to whistle.

Gib's dilated pupils and spaced-out look were replaced by the
flickering spark of intelligence in his eyes. There was someone at
home inside that head. He frowned, rolled his eyes; there wasn't a
thing he did without my complete amazement and gratitude.

A miracle? Yes, but God didn't zap this child and make him
well. He made us work for it and learn from it. Blind faith got us
to Switzerland because we were scared out of our wits. If you don't
have the sense to know when God's helping you and trust Him
completely no matter what, you may never get another chance.

—

In the spring of that year, Shirley MacLaine's book, "Out on a Limb," was made into a television movie. The book was about her spiritual journey to accept reincarnation, divine guidance and purpose, out of body experiences, and aliens. The movie prompted skeptical laughter, but it also prompted discussion.

One day I was talking on the phone with Gibby's teacher, and she asked me what I thought of the movie.

"Well," I said cautiously, "I've never had any psychic experiences, so I can't relate to her story, but I'm also certain that I don't know everything there is to know."

"Have you ever had an out-of-body experience?" she asked.

"No, but I don't doubt that it happens," I replied.

"Well, I have," she answered and proceeded to tell me her story. She had been napping on a wintry Sunday afternoon while her husband and daughters built a snowman in the yard. She floated above her body until she became aware of her family. As she floated toward them and out over the yard, she went with her curiosity and flew over the snowy countryside until she came to a warm, sunny beach. She walked in the sand, enjoying herself and watching other people at the beach, until a little blond boy approached her. He explained that his name was Donald. He had many allergies that made him sick, and he would soon be one of her students. They talked and walked in the sand, enjoying the warmth. Pretty soon he said he had to leave her and ran off over a dune.

She noticed that other people didn't seem to notice her, and she became curious about that. Her plan was to approach the next person, stand directly in front of him, and ask a question. When she did, and he didn't answer, she knew she was dreaming. She felt herself fall into her body with a thud.

I was stunned by her story. "Oh, my gosh. Gibby's given name is Donald," I whispered.

"What? I never put that together. But how could it have been him? That was years ago," she said.

"Because when you're out of body you can choose a period from how you looked during that lifetime," I said, thinking of my classes with Elaine.

"You're right," she agreed. "I suppose it could have been Gibby. I'll have to think about it a bit more." I thought it was a definite possibility. Gibby slept so hard during his naptime; sometimes he could not be awakened. Other times he would wake up insisting that he was flying like an airplane.

It was a big event in Detroit when Pope John Paul visited in 1987. Don and I watched the late evening news. The Pope arrived at the Detroit Metropolitan Airport, entered a helicopter, and flew to the cardinal's residence for his stay.

Knowing how much Gibby loved airplanes and how much he loved cathedrals, I said to Don, "Boy, if Gib really does go out of body, I wonder if he's there watching all of this commotion."

"Don't know. Interesting idea. Let's go to bed, though. I'm exhausted, and the boys will be up early," Don said.

We turned off all the lights, checked the doors, drank some water, and climbed the stairs to our room.

"I'll take Gibby to the bathroom," Don offered. Every night we tried to see whether we could help him make it through a dry night by taking him to the toilet. He was a chronic bed-wetter, and he slept so hard, he never stood a chance of awakening on his own. He had recently taken to sleeping on the floor to avoid wetting his bed, so we put rubber pants over his training pants.

I was just climbing into bed when Don entered the room with that quizzical look of his.

"Damn, that kid is weird sometimes," he said.

"Why?"

"I could not wake him up. I stood him in front of the toilet and he was limp. I stood him up, coaxing him to wake up, and he was deadweight. Finally I gave up and, just as I put him back into bed, he said, 'People flying in helicopters, Dad.' Now how did he know that?"

"I'm telling you, this little guy is something else," I laughed.

"Well you're telling me. It creeps me out sometimes," Don exclaimed.

—

At the close of the school year, at Gibby's Individual Educational Plan (IEP) meeting, the team acknowledged his improved status, but they weren't sure where to place him or how to qualify him for the second grade. After much discussion they thought that labeling him with learning disabilities due to developmental delay would place him in a special education situation for extra help, and there would be a smaller teacher-student ratio.

I was hesitant about labeling him just yet. I knew he was improving from the Swiss treatment and wanted to buy him some time to develop. I also felt he needed to compare himself to other students and learn from them.

We were participating in a horseback-riding program for physically handicapped children that helped Gib's posture and balance. I also knew the teachers were preparing to release us due to his marked improvements. By chance, I overheard two women talking about a new private school in the area that offered a smaller classroom ratio. I made a mental note to check it out. If Gib needed a smaller teacher-student ratio and the public system wasn't sure how to classify him, I'd explore my options.

I narrowed my choices to three schools. One was a Montessori school, another was a private school specializing in learning disabilities, and the third was a new, local private academy. When staff members at the academy evaluated Gibby, I felt connected immediately. I gave the headmistress the short version of our Swiss experience and expressed my need for a learning environment that would nurture Gibby's development, allowing him the room he needed to catch up from the illness years.

"Is this your school?" I asked her.

"Yes it is. Why do you ask?"

"It is always interesting for me to meet people who are realizing their dreams," I said. Gibby's evaluation was completed, and we were preparing to part ways.

"I can offer you a place here, but I would need to hold your son back a year. My first graders are quite advanced, and I think Gibby would have trouble catching up to them," she stated. "Not a problem. I know his development is delayed by two years. You can't come through an illness like that without repercussions. Let me discuss this with my husband and get back with you." I thanked her for a wonderful afternoon.

I was having the toughest time making my decision. The private school was geared toward kids like Gib, but the teachers were experienced with middle and high school-aged children. They were in the process of starting an elementary school. The academy was wonderful, but the school was only two years old and lacked basic amenities like a playground, library, and computer laboratory. Montessori was looking like the best possibility at that point.

One morning my dear friend Lil called. "I woke up this morning with the strongest impression that you need to visit those schools spontaneously," she said. "Don't tell them you're coming by; just show up and see what happens. Bring me the boys and just go."

"Are you sure?" I was trying to adapt myself to this opportunity, mentally switching gears for a day that had been planned for something else.

"Yes, I insist. Do it today. Just get yourself ready and drop the boys off. I'll get them dressed and feed them breakfast."

"Wow. OK, I'll be there in a half hour," I said. "Oh, and Lil, thank you. You are wonderful."

The spontaneous visit was enlightening. The Montessori school administrator flat out refused to let me observe a classroom. This was upsetting to their routine and not necessary for them. They were decidedly unfriendly, and I knew instantly this was not our learning environment. The private school didn't have an operating lower elementary division, but I was welcome to observe their middle school from the hallway. The academy's administrator was happy to see me and welcomed me into a first-grade classroom.

"Children," announced the teacher, "this is Mrs. Topping, and she is visiting our school today because she is considering our school for her little boy."

"What is your little boy's name?" inquired one child.

"His name is Don, but we use his middle name and call him Gibby," I answered.

"Children, let's sing a song for Mrs. Topping," the teacher said, and they broke into a song in French. I sat for a while observing the respectful dynamics in the classroom. Then I left, thanking the children for sharing their time with me. I looked back at the school before driving away and considered the lack of amenities. "Oh well," I decided. "I'll just have to help fundraise for those things." I was smitten with the spirit of the population in that school. My decision was made.

Over the summer the boys received their school physical examinations. Nathaniel was starting kindergarten at the local public grade school, and Gib was going off to the academy. At the conclusion of their examinations, the doctor entered the room to discuss the results. She was well-pleased with Gib's improvements.

"See, Mom," she said. "I told you it would be all right. He seems to be doing just great."

I looked at her like she was delusional. Where had she been during all this? I'd kept her informed of all the testing, made sure results were sent to her, had a yearly physical examination for Gib, and considered her part of the team. Here she was just assuming he had developed his way into the normal range.

"Really. Let me tell you why he's doing so great. I took him to Switzerland to a doctor who is affiliated with the Louis Pasteur Labs and a member of the World Health Organization for a treatment to rebuild his immune system using live-cell therapy."

She stumbled back against the wall with her arms akimbo and a shocked look on her face.

"What?" she sputtered indignantly. "Why on earth would you ever leave this country for medical treatment when we offer the finest medicine possible?"

"Because I'd have to be pretty stupid to think that the U. S. is the only country making medical breakthroughs in the world. Also, my child can't wait 10 years for a treatment in Europe to become mainstream here." I was a bit irritated, but I knew it wasn't her fault.

This was an education for every person involved. I launched into a brief explanation of the treatment.

"Do you know," I added, "while I was in the doctor's office, a famous medical school was consulting the doctor on the uses of human placenta in treating cystic fibrosis. This was a top drawer organization, and we owed it to our son to offer him every viable opportunity."

"Do you have any literature I can read?" she asked quietly.

"Yes. I have some literature, and I can also provide you with our doctor's contact information. Our allergist has already been in discussion with him."

She seemed subdued as she walked away. I was beyond worrying what she thought of our actions. I was confident that our intentions had been pure. It was a holistic approach to healing, and most importantly, it worked. There was no denying the obvious.

—

Poor Danny was worsening, and I was guilt-ridden. Gibby was thriving and making improvements while his best friend was going in the opposite direction. Barb was beside herself with grief.

"I just don't know what else I can do," she worried. "Every time I take him to a doctor, he examines him, says he can't help and refers us to another."

"Doctors are fine if you fall within the normal ranges of the bell curve, but the minute you hit the fringes, they don't have any answers," I sympathized.

"I called the State of Michigan toxicology lab and spoke to the head toxicologist who said to take Dan to the children's hospital," she said. "It is his opinion that they have the best toxicologist. I don't know what I'll do if this doesn't help him. I can't just sit here and watch this." I knew that Danny was no longer talking or walking, that he drooled incessantly and feebly cried, "Help me." It was truly heart-wrenching.

Blood work revealed a high level of mercury in Danny's liver. The doctors made a plan to chelate the mercury to help expel it, but Danny's body was unable to rid itself of the toxin, and it all stayed in the bloodstream. Dan suffered brain damage and was left in a near vegetative state. Barb was bereft with grief.

"I know it's not their fault. His body is what it is. They tried to help; it just didn't work. My poor little guy, there doesn't seem to be any help out there for him." I could tell this was the end of the line for his parents. I distinctly heard defeat in Barb's voice.

This poor little tyke was not having an easy time with life. Barb had become his foster parent when he was a baby because his birth mother was an alcoholic and drug abuser. When Danny returned to his birth mother, she lost her parenting privileges for good when she tossed him off the porch steps in a fit of anger. Barb and her husband eagerly stepped forward to adopt the little baby with whom they'd fallen in love. Their two birth children were used to foster siblings, as their parents sought to make a difference in the lives of others. They loved Danny well.

After receiving his vaccines he began having seizures, and the seizure medicine caused him to lose his ability to walk. It had been one loss after another until he reached this unavoidable outcome. We were all heartsick to realize that for the remainder of Danny's life we would watch him wither away.

One beautiful summer afternoon, my phone rang and it was Barb. I was anxious to hear how Danny was doing.

"Hey, kiddo. How's Dan?"

"They've taken him away from me."

"What? Who? Barb, what's going on?" I was confused.

"The hospital. They're taking away our parental rights. Can you believe it? They think I poisoned him." She croaked on the word poison.

"Barb. ..."

"It's a case of, 'Damn, we've really screwed up now. Well, wait a minute. That mercury had to come from somewhere. She must have given it to him.' Can you believe it? This is our life they're playing with."

"What?" I breathed into the phone. I felt my legs cave under me, and I sank to the floor in my family room. "Barb, I don't understand this. How can they do such a heinous thing?"

"They've conveniently labeled me with Munchausen syndrome by proxy. Isn't that something? They think I'm breaking open thermometers or something and feeding him the mercury. How could I possibly do something like that do my little guy?"

I sat on the floor cradling the phone in my lap. I was numb with shock, and tears were streaming down my cheeks.

"They're going to release him from the hospital to the care of foster parents. Can you imagine how he'll feel? He's blind from the brain stem damage, and they're sending him to a strange house with people he doesn't even know. Poor Danny, he didn't do anything. Poor, poor Danny." I could hear Barb crying.

"This is the most heinous thing I've ever heard of. How can they just arbitrarily accuse you of being mentally ill?"

"They found out we went to Switzerland for medical treatment. That's supposed to prove how unfit we are."

"What?" I fairly shouted into the phone. "How could they know that?"

"The school psychologist, that's how. She is a friend of the social worker on this case, and she took it upon herself to call and share her information. Remember when she sat next to a friend of yours at a conference? When they found they had you in common, your friend said something like, 'Isn't it wild how they took their sons to Switzerland for a medical treatment?' When she heard about Danny's predicament in the hospital, she called her friend and said, 'I'll tell you how unstable the mother is. She took her child to Europe for an unorthodox medical treatment.' So you were right in the end. There isn't anyone we can trust. They're using it as proof of my mental instability."

"Oh my God, Barb. I'm so sorry." I was really crying by now. "I feel so responsible."

"No, don't. It was going to come out sooner or later anyway."

"But we didn't do anything wrong. It isn't an unorthodox treatment. It's something available to the rest of the world. It's mainstream in Europe. Isn't it our right to avail ourselves of medical treatments? Why must we pay the price for their ignorance?" I was indignant. "Isn't doofus betraying client confidentiality?"

"I never had a conversation with any of the hospital people about this," Barb said.

"Exactly. Aren't they just acting on rumor?"

"They asked me if we'd done this, and I said yes."

"Well, I don't think much of Mrs. Smart. How does she know her facts are straight? She knows nothing, and she's trashing your integrity? I'm finding this a little unethical on her part." I was angry.

"Yeah, well." Barb sounded exhausted. "Who am I? I'm just a mother trying to get help for her son. Do you want to hear something really sad? The proof they offered was that Dan wasn't my birth child. He's 'just adopted,' like I care less about him than my birth children."

"That's just evil."

"When you love someone," Barb continued, "what does it matter where he came from? I didn't give birth to my husband, either, but I love him. Just because I didn't give birth to Danny doesn't mean he's not mine. He's been mine since the moment I first held him, the same as my other children."

"This conversation can't be happening. I want to wake up now."

"Oh, it's happening," she muttered. "My poor little guy. Why is this happening to such an innocent, ill little boy? Doesn't he have enough pain? I just don't understand this. The doctors weren't responsible for his body not working. They were just trying to help him; I know that. We wouldn't have pressed charges."

We talked for hours. I felt awful that my friend had been the conduit of information, but on the other hand, the psychologist had deceived her into talking. Barb was generous, not blaming anyone. She just wanted her little boy home to her loving arms. The hospital wasn't even allowing unsupervised visits.

In time, Danny was released to the foster family while Barb and Mark hired an attorney to help them get their boy home. Somehow the press found out and the story hit the front pages of the local newspapers. I was absolutely horrified to read these articles because they were inaccurate and misleading. Here was a group of professionals doing a character assassination on someone not even tried by the courts, and they were putting it out to the public as *fait accompli*. I was horrified at the pain this was creating. The attorney kept focused on the case. Barb and Mark waited patiently for their supervised visits with their son, a blind quadriplegic by now, while I ranted and raved about injustice. To make matters worse, someone in an authority position managed to contact the birth mother and notify her that the "abuse case" in the newspapers involved her child. Now Barb was receiving calls from this woman, who was crying and carrying on that she only gave up her parental rights so her baby could have a better life, not a worse one. Barb kindly reminded the girl that, if she hadn't been abusive, Danny would never have been in the foster care situation. I could not fathom this betrayal of confidentiality. My heart went out to Barb and Mark's teenage children as well.

—

Through my travels I learned of a program affiliated with the Institutes for the Achievement of Human Potential. Founded by Dr. Glenn Doman, a researcher specializing in childhood brain development, the organization fosters methods of accelerated childhood learning based on his studies.

A group of parents in the Flint area sponsored a specialist who came into the area to evaluate our special needs children and recommend a program for us to work on within our homes. The evaluation showed that Gib had mixed dominance; his left ear was dominant, his right eye was also, his hands were ambidextrous, and he led with his left foot. The specialist told me this confusion was causing Gib to file knowledge away in areas of his brain that were hard to find and access.

He suggested getting Gib's dominance reoriented to one side, with the eye dominance being the determining factor. I was instructed to play music for him with an earjack in the right ear. I also needed to train him to step off with his right foot.

Another problem was Gib's inability to creep. Since the brain is basically a computer, skipping an important development step could lead to a host of learning problems. I was encouraged to take him home and teach him how to creep on the floor.

Since I was 8 months pregnant, creeping was impossible. I tried to position his alternating arm-leg pose and coax him into pulling forward, but it wasn't working. I tried everything I could think of until I was at my wits' end with frustration. Don picked up his phone to hear, "Come home tonight. I need you to teach this kid to creep."

"What?" Don laughed.

"This is not a joke. I cannot get creeping across to this kid and this damn belly is in my way. How am I supposed to get on the floor and do a G.I. Joe creep with this big baby belly? Do you know how useless and hideous I am?" I was peeved. "I'm educated to help companies with their business systems, not educate children on the merits of creeping! Can you believe the absurdity of my life? I can't freaking creep. Whose idea was this parenthood thing anyway? I quit." I was on my way to a major meltdown.

"OK, OK. Just relax. I'll come home and teach the kid to creep."

"I'm serious. I'm quitting."

"You can't quit," Don said simply.

"Who says? I'm writing up my resignation when I get off the phone," I huffed.

"Well I'm not accepting it. Now find something else to do until I get home. I will get on the floor and teach the kid to creep."

Well, they never said parenting would be easy. They just didn't say how absurd it could become.

—

The time for birthing our baby was upon us, and I was worrying that my angst might upset "Celeste," as we had taken to calling her. I was certainly a basket case worrying about Gib, worrying about Danny, worrying about every part of parenting. My parents were concerned. The day my labor started, my dad decided to help me can tomatoes. Mom joined us as we toiled away the day, happily teasing each other and talking. Mom picked up the boys from their schools and brought them home. As the last jar was capped, I sat down to admire the fruits of our labor when labor did indeed begin.

Horrendous storms rocked the area that night, and by morning, when we drove to the hospital, most of the area was without electrical power. Although the hospital was on auxiliary power, it was low on staff members. Don and the doctor had to wheel me into delivery themselves, crashing into door jams and gurneys on the way. Our little Vanessa made a perfect entrance, and I was over the moon with joy. If the other births had gone as well, we would have had six kids.

Our lives were finally smoothing out. Gib continued to improve from the treatment boosters. Don's shingles were under control and he was benefiting from his treatment with great vim and vigor. Nat was the jovial big brother for Gib and Vanessa, and the baby was problem-free. I was enjoying parenthood for the first time.

Life was good, yet at the back of my brain I was tormented by Barb's situation. Her family was just as deserving of happiness, and they were so strained. We waited a long time before their case was ready for court. I was worried about my tentative happiness; how long would it last? Would people take Gib away from us, too? Would future medical treatment be denied to him because doctors thought we were nuts? Testifying was unavoidable. We'd been through so much together; I had to do the right thing for Dan.

The lawyers took our deposition. Yes, we'd taken our child to Switzerland for a medical treatment, but the doctor had top drawer credentials, and the treatment had existed in Europe for 40 years. Yes, the treatment helped our son; the school evaluations could attest to his improvement. Besides, Don had received the treatment as well, with no ill effects.

When the case went before the judge, he reviewed the papers and dismissed the Swiss treatment as an issue in the case. He ruled that Barb was guilty of medical neglect because she discontinued the phenobarbital treatment. (A toxicologist knew that the phenobarbital gave Danny hyperbilirubinism, but that information didn't make it to the hearing.) Despite the phenobarbital finding, Danny was returned to his loving parents. It was mind-numbing.

When Nat began kindergarten at our neighborhood school, I was thrilled. I had attended that elementary school as a child. It was one of the premier schools in the district, and the principal was reputed to be absolutely wonderful. Imagine my dismay when he called to tell me Natty would have to be bused to another school. He informed me that the classroom was over its limit in size. I was irritated to learn that other neighbors around us had been accepted. I'd had enough of this stuff. I interviewed with the principal and pled my case.

He attempted to maneuver me into an emotional state to gain control of the situation. I'd studied transactional analysis, thank you very much, and I was not going to lose control of this process.

"I feel your pain, Mrs. Topping. It must be so hard with your other son's handicap," he said sympathetically.

"Yes, which is exactly why I'm adamant that I not be forced to bus another of my children into another neighborhood."

"Our capacity is full. We simply cannot accommodate you."

"So your decision is final?"

"Yes, I'm afraid it is," he answered.

"Then you have no issue with me discussing this with your supervisor?"

He looked surprised. "Well, no. I suppose I don't."

"Thank you for your time." I left his office.

After having a brief conversation with his supervisor, and giving a full description of our circumstances, we were accepted to the school of our choice. This should have been the happy ending, but it wasn't. The teacher complained loud and clear, at every opportunity, that she had 33 students instead of 29, and she didn't have an aide. I quickly stepped forward to be the best parent she had. I was room mother, and I was a reading aide. I recruited a pianist for the Christmas pageant, and I organized field trips. I was at the school so much I noticed Natty helping other students with their math problems. I also noticed that most of his time was spent doodling drawings.

Finally, at a conference where I was receiving his glowing report, I asked why the teacher never stopped to comment on his work. Surely he deserved some praise, a moment's worth of recognition in the course of a day.

"How can I when I must attend to the problem students?" she retorted. When Don came home, I simply stated that we had a problem.

"If he continues to skate through and never learns to work, we will have a classic underachiever on our hands," I rationalized. "I'm thankful he's that intelligent and not having problems, but what good will it be if he doesn't know how to apply himself to work?" Don agreed. It was time to move him to the academy as well.

The day the academy's headmistress evaluated Nat, she took me aside to question his placement within the school. Nat sat off to one side, doodling.

"I'm concerned about placing him with my first graders for next year. Even though they are currently kindergarteners, most of them are reading," she said.

"Mom, can I have some scissors?" Nat interrupted. The headmistress supplied him with a pair, and we resumed talking.

"He isn't reading yet because he simply isn't interested in it," I said. "The pre-reading skills are in place; he just isn't motivated. He's interested in other things right now. I think holding him back would be a mistake for him."

"Momma, look what I made," Nat interrupted again.

We both looked at him. He'd cut four triangles out that were joined at the top. At the base of one triangle was a folded square. When he joined the triangles together at their apex and attached the square as a base, he was holding a 3-D pyramid, complete with hieroglyphics. "Can I please have some tape?" he asked.

Our mouths fell open. The headmistress grabbed her tape for him to finish his project, which he then gave her. Nat was placed in the proper class.

CHAPTER EIGHT

We are not human beings on a spiritual journey. We are
spiritual beings on a human journey.
Stephen Covey

That fall I high-tailed it to a meeting of the Michigan Metaphysical
Society for English psychic Mrs. Fall's annual visit. I was very
committed to my self-education in this area. I was maintaining an
open mind to things I did not know much about, but I certainly
was not being gullible.

Most of what I learned enhanced my traditional Christian
beliefs. I already had proof positive that prayers were answered and
direction was given, and that an open mind could yield the correct
results as evidenced by our experiences with Dr. Burke. Life was
about learning and discovery, and I was fervent about filling the gaps
in my knowledge. This was during a time before revelations about
quantum physics, black holes, and quarks. My reality was a little boy
who was language-impaired but could read my mind, who told me
of places he flew to at night and warned me of dangers.

My appointment with Mrs. Fall that year was particularly
enlightening. Besides discussing the usual deceased relatives that I
didn't personally know but could verify as authentic, she told me that
my grandfather continued to assist me. He said he was very proud of
my progress on this side, and that I was the 100th Monkey. When
I said I didn't understand, she went on to explain.

"The 100th Monkey is an old parable," she began. "The 100th Monkey gets the idea to wash his fruit before eating it. When he begins to do just that, the other monkeys laugh and mock him. But he continues on, and before he knows what's happening, the others try washing their fruit, too. Soon all the monkeys have changed their behavior and it's commonplace. And the 100th Monkey is YOU!" she exclaimed, looking directly at me. I was stunned by her intensity and left with much to think about.

I began meditating weekly as I sought a way to manage the stress of three youngsters. The kids were thriving, and I was beginning to believe I could handle this motherhood gig. I was so appreciative of where I was in life. I was so new to this happy feeling that I was fearful of it. I kept thinking of the book "Flowers for Algernon," a story about a retarded man who was made a genius, only to have the treatment reverse itself. My mind tormented me that we too might suffer a reverse. The meditation and prayer helped me unload the stress, thank God for his mercy, and resolve to put my best efforts back into life.

—

My friend Lil had supported me emotionally through so much of the chaos of those illness years. We also babysat for each other's children so that I could bowl in a ladies league and she could join her husband on his day off.

One evening we had a phone conversation about reincarnation. I'd studied it quite a bit and had an experience during a meditation that amazed me. I saw myself as an Indian in the northern woods. I couldn't tell whether I was male or female, but I walked through the dense forest dappled with sunlight. I could virtually smell the damp earth and feel its coolness. I approached a small settlement of three to four bark homes with the smoke of a couple of cooking fires wafting skyward. Two women worked over the campfire, and another woman approached them. When they all looked up at me, white light shown from their eyes, and I knew they were my mom and two of my sisters from my current lifetime.

Before I could speak to them, I was in a rowboat on a river, and as I banked the boat and disembarked, I looked at my feet. My shoes had spats over them. I wore pinstriped trousers, a vest and jacket and was adorned with a beautiful gold watch fob. I strolled along a dirt road toward the village and was amazed at the quiet of it. Children played with hoops in a park, shops facing its periphery. The sounds of the children carried a long way; it was that quiet. Chirping birds sang loudly. It was a gentler time. As I walked along a street and prepared to turn the corner away from town, I saw a rotund banker standing on the sidewalk in front of his bank, talking to a woman with children. He was foreclosing on her mortgage and telling her it was nothing personal, it was only business. When he looked at me to nod a greeting, I saw the same curious white light. I recognized another one of my sisters from this life who, coincidentally, suffers financial problems herself in this life.

I walked a bit, listened to kids squeal and dogs bark, enjoyed the sunshine and felt full of self-satisfaction. I was full of ego and pride. The house I approached was a two-story brick home with wood trim, a fenced yard, and big shade trees. I entered the house. I was very satisfied with myself as a provider.

A center hallway led to the back of the house, and on either side were a parlor and a living room. A woman approached me from the back to greet me at the door. She was plump, short, dressed in brown, and wore an apron. Her light brown hair was pulled back in a bun. She was quieting the two little ones, encouraging them to go play, as though I were too important to be bothered with children. When she looked at me, there was that white light behind the eyes again. I recognized her as Don! I knew that in that life I had been too full of myself to appreciate her position. I never considered her needs; I was a complete chauvinist.

Lil and I laughed about that because my working career had been spent fighting that very attitude. Here I was, after all that, a stay-at-home mother when it wasn't cool to be one. Lil and I were the only stay-at-home moms in the neighborhood, and I was now dealing with reverse discrimination. At least Don was empathetic to my position.

"You know what?" I added. "There are times when I'm talking to you and I see that same white light around your eyes."

"I'm not surprised. I'm sure we had a life together, too," Lil laughed.

"Really? What are you picking up?" I was intrigued. Lil's intuition had always been reliable.

"I see myself being driven in a horse-drawn buggy to visit you. I'm riding up a long, dirt drive circular drive in front of a large manor home. You're a little girl, an only child of an unhappy marriage, and I'm concerned about you because my daughter is ill and not nurturing you properly," she began. "We're in England, and I see you grown up and being courted for marriage. He rides up the drive on a big gray horse. I can't figure out what war he's going off to, but he's wearing a red sash. Wait a minute while I try to see who it is." Lil was silent for a few seconds before continuing. "Why, it's Don! He loves you and promises to return, but he never does. It's so sad. You never do marry. You end up caring for the villagers when they are sick."

"Ha! When I first met Don he always insisted that he wouldn't live to see 30 years of age. It was all rather morbid, and I was glad when he did reach 30. He never mentioned it after that." I thought this was an interesting little coincidence.

"Your father in this life was your father then. He and my daughter hate each other," Lil continued. "Your mother in this life is the housekeeper. She lives in a cottage on the estate with your brother as her son in that time, too." I thought what an interesting imagination Lil had and just sat back enjoying the story. "Oh my," she giggled. "They are having an affair! The housekeeper really resents not being the 'lady of the manor.' She feels she deserves that place."

This tidbit caught my attention. When I was a teenager, my mom would always laugh at our family money woes and say, "I was meant to be the lady of the manor," which always seemed odd to me. My sense was that she wasn't kidding; she meant it. Surely this was just another coincidence.

"I can't tell who my daughter is," Lil mused. "Give me a minute," and she trailed off to silence. "It's funny, but all I can see is someone who has fallen down a hole and is looking up at the sky."

I was dumbstruck. "Lil," I gasped hoarsely, "my grandmother fell down a well in England when she was two or three years old. A crossbar caught her and broke her collarbone, and she remembered looking up to see her rescuers." Lil had never met my grandmother.

"Then she is my daughter."

"Funny, but it's believable because she and I have always been close. It's always been a family mystery why she and my dad disliked each other so much. Mom said it was instant, on first sight of each other.

That story always stayed with Lil and me. My nickname for her was Granny, much to the curiosity of our children. I wasn't sure what I thought of these so-called past life stories. They must be the result of active imaginations, sprinkled with coincidences. Now it seems funny to me that the brain tries to explain things in the terms with which it is familiar. How could one ever experience growth with that much self-doubt? I always trusted my intuition; in fact I was usually really sorry the times that I didn't heed it. Now I wondered what exactly intuition was.

I started to regard my intuition seriously. I thought everyone had it and trusted it. It was shocking to me that people could deny its existence. When I was a little girl, my mother had always encouraged me to listen to the little voice inside my head that warned me of dangers. She had felt it was God's way of talking to us and keeping us safe. Since I was cued to acknowledge it at an early age, I just accepted it was as normal as my eyesight or my hearing. As an adult, I took it for granted.

Don and I once were at an office party when he asked if I wanted to meet a client. I looked across the room to the man in question, and I saw darkness all around him. This had never happened before in my life, and I was puzzled, as well as repelled.

"No way, thank you very much. He's evil."

Don laughed. "Well, there are some who wouldn't argue that. Come on."

"No, I mean it. I'm not going anywhere near that man. If you need to talk to him, you go." I was adamant. Years later one of the guys who worked with Don found the client in a New York City bookstore buying books on Satanism. Like I said, my intuition was reliable.

Another time I was lying on my sofa reading a magazine when I received the sudden impulse to drive over to Grandma's house and get the garden hose out of the basement for her. I put the baby in the car, drove to Grandma's and announced, "I'm here to get the garden hose out of the basement for you."

She looked at me in puzzlement. "Did your mother call you?"

"No, why?"

"We were just talking about you this morning. Mom said she was going to call you to see if you'd get it out of the basement for me."

"Huh. That's funny," I answered. Grandma just kept looking at me oddly.

Gib was doing the same to me. In fact, I would test him on it when we drove in the car. I'd think Blue House, Blue House, Blue House, and he'd say, "OK, Blue House!"

To prove my point to Don one Sunday morning, I said, "OK, let's try this little experiment. Let's just say we're going to buy donuts and see what happens." It was a random idea because we rarely ate the things. They would kill my stomach whenever I did eat them. We were in our second-floor bedroom; the boys were playing in the basement on the other end of the house. Almost instantly, after declaring we should buy donuts, we heard feet running up the stairs before the door crashed open. Gibby yelled, "OK! Let's buy some donuts!" Don just laughed as he grabbed his car keys to run to the store.

—

Now that both our sons were going to private school, we began to think of a new home with easier freeway access to aid Don in his commute into the city. We found an area being newly developed that got us excited enough to move. Don and I met with the architects, signed the paperwork, and put our house on the market to sell.

"Gee, Don," I fussed, I'm feeling a bit overwhelmed with these three children to be building one house and selling the other."

"Don't worry. I'll handle it," were Don's famous last words. He had no sooner uttered those words than the winds of change heightened to tornado force.

Don's father was diagnosed with cancer that summer, so we traveled to Missouri with the kids every vacation day and holiday. Time with Dad was precious, and the children had a short time to build memories of him to last a lifetime.

Dad had bought a cabin on a lake, which was a wonderful setting for the family. The first time I stood by the water, I realized a dream that I'd had a few weeks earlier. In my dream a paddleboat that was overloaded with children capsized, and I felt the terror of the adults as they tried to retrieve all of the kids. As I pulled back from the scene, I saw that other residents on the shoreline were panicking and trying to get their watercraft into the water to assist the others. I described the scene to my sister-in-law, who looked at me with her mouth open.

"How could you possibly know that?" she said. "You are describing exactly what happened two weeks ago. Dad and I watched from the shore, helpless because we didn't have a boat yet. It was dreadful."

"I'm not sure how I know. I just dreamt it," I answered, but she gave me the weirdest look. I was overloaded with the evidence of my first premonition. While I dreamt it, my reasoning told me to pay attention and that I was seeing reality. This was too strange. I quickly dismissed the experience. I was too overwhelmed to do otherwise.

Don and Dad enjoyed working on our building plans for the new house together, calculating stress loads and other concerns. Natty was just a kindergartener, and he coaxed his dad into building a model of the house out of foam core. Nat was the one to discover a roof problem over one bedroom. Dad and Grandpa had a good laugh about a 5-year-old correcting the architects.

My beloved grandmother was beginning to fail as well. She would constantly call me for reassurances when she felt her deceased loved ones around. "Grandma, why do you think I understand any of this?" I'd ask.

"Because you and Gib are psychic," she would answer.

"What?" I'd laugh. "It's the first I've heard of it."

I tried to lighten her mood. She wasn't ready to die and resented the ministrations of her dead relatives. One late night her telephone rang, and when she picked it up, no one was on the other line. Her deceased son's GI number flashed through her mind. She was convinced he had tried to contact her. Another time a teacup fell to the floor from a display shelf on the wall. When she picked up a slip of paper that fell from the cup to examine it, she saw that it was her brother's obituary.

These episodes sent her into anxiety states. I never told her about the shadow I would see around me that I took to calling Grandpa; I was that convinced he was around.

Grandma was still living alone. There was no way she would ever leave the house she helped build, she said. My mom, sisters, and I helped her with a myriad of problems and tasks. We were giving her house a thorough spring-cleaning one Saturday when I experienced another premonition. I stood standing at her kitchen sink washing the dishes and saw, in my mind, a picture of her falling down the basement stairs. Puzzled, I turned to look at the back door landing, just where it headed downstairs.

"What's wrong?" my sister asked.

"Nothing." I wasn't sure what had just happened. The mind is curious. We can reason away anything. I had nothing to reference this to, so I dismissed it.

A few days later, Grandma decided to get a hammer from the basement and fell down the stairs, breaking her hip. An alert neighbor noticed the living room lights were not on when it got dark and called my mother.

Once while I was visiting Grandma in the hospital, the nurse had her out of bed and sitting in a chair. She had to run for something and asked me to support Grandma until her return. I stood in front of her, holding her upright, and listened to her moan.

"I love you, Grandma," I said.

She emitted more moans while she tried to open her eyes for me. I felt like we were being observed and turned to look at the corner of the room. No one was there.

"Grandma? I love you. Can you hear me?" I quickly turned to see if the nurse was behind me, but no one was there. "Man, I'm losing it," I muttered to myself.

"Grandma! I love you!" I was persistent about getting through to her.

"Eh?" she asked, opening her big blue eyes to look right into mine; our heads were that close.

"I love you."

"Hey, I love you, too," she agreed. As her eyes drifted from mine, she glanced around the room.

"The nurse ran out for a minute. She asked me to support you in this chair until she can return," I told her. Her eyes settled on the spooky corner and narrowed, then glanced at me.

"Who are they and what are they doing here?" she asked.

"I don't know, Grandma. I feel them, too."

The nurse returned and the moment was lost. A few days later, when I'd returned for another visit, Grandma's condition was much improved.

"You know," she said, "Dale was here yesterday." I looked at her in puzzlement, because her son had died 10 years previously. I thought maybe she'd gone a little batty.

"He was?" I decided to humor her. "What did he want?"

"I don't know, honestly. I told him to go away; I'm not a quitter like he was."

"Grandma!" I admonished. "He couldn't help it; he had an embolism in his aorta."

"Yes, but I'm not ready to die, so I told him he could just leave." My goodness, I'd always known she was feisty, but this took the cake. When she was released to a nursing home, I commuted weekly to visit her. Mom was the only child to attend to Grandma's needs, so I picked up the slack to help her. I always felt like Grandma's daughter, anyway.

In the midst of the chaos that was our life, I had a random revelation about the new house we were building. The thought kept occurring to me that we were building on an Indian burial ground.

91

I thought this was truly the craziest thing I'd experienced to date. The idea just would not quit. I thought Indians built platforms for their dead, so I decided to squash that thought.

The day we moved into our new home was a scene from a crazy movie. Our sales contract on the old house required us to be out, and we told our builder we were moving our stuff in. There wasn't enough room in the moving van for the garage stuff, so Don was irritated at having to hire another truck. When the moving van left, Don directed me to get to the new house to prepare the way. He was a bit short-tempered, so my sister and girlfriend who were helping us hopped into the car with me to escape.

When we drove up to the new house, I couldn't believe my eyes. Scaffolding blocked the front door, carpet layers were finishing bedrooms, plumbers were in the basement doing a pressure test. As I looked down the center hallway, I counted nine workmen. I had never seen this much action on our build job. This was unfathomable. Today, of all days, they all decide to work? The building supervisor walked up to me.

"Hey Sue," he tossed out.

"Hey, hell," I said, pushing him out of earshot of the workmen. "What are you doing? We told you we were moving our stuff in today. What is this?"

"Well, I can't help it that they all decided to show up today."

"Is this their idea of a joke? Ha, ha, the homeowners think they're moving in when?" I gasped. "Listen, you'd better have an answer before Don and that moving van arrive."

It was too late. I could hear the truck shifting gears as it climbed the hill.

The looks on the moving men's faces were priceless. Everyone stood outside looking at our house and its plethora of workmen like it was one of the true wonders of the world.

"Listen, my men can't work around all this," the lead mover said. "We'll take your stuff back to the warehouse and return Monday morning to unload it." As they drove away with all of our earthly possessions, I shuddered to think that I might never see those things again. Our clothing was packed away on that truck, and we were forced to miss the black tie gala our developer was giving that night. We bunked at my parent's home, and Don had to borrow business attire from Dad so that he could address a client meeting Monday morning.

I heard from the builder that the black tie event we'd been forced to miss had been a terrific party. I missed hearing from the other residents all the local legends that the mansion was haunted and that this area had been an Indian burial ground.

"What? I thought Indians disposed of their dead on platforms. I wouldn't have built here if I'd know it was a cemetery."

"Oh, I doubt it's really true," he laughed. I wasn't convinced, having lived with my random thoughts for the past eight months. I was truly perplexed.

Most of the first year in our home was fraught with building problems, and now Don had a new work assignment that required a lot of foreign travel as he began to globalize his accounts. I began to dust off my old assertive self to get about the business of hounding our builder to complete the stupid house.

That good old boy network is truly aggravating. The boys hang together, compile their list of excuses for their negligence, and really use the shallowest of explanations for dealing with you such as your female hormones, as if they're experts on that subject. They wait until your husband finally appears. Then they get serious.

I was exhausted from this haphazard process. It had been a long six months of fighting to get the details of the house finished. I knew I needed to up the stakes.

"Denny," I warned the builder. "When the weather turns hot and my air conditioner still isn't installed, you'd better worry."

"Ah, Sue, it'll be there. Trust me." How many times had I heard that promise? Unbeknownst to him, I'd already done my homework. Sure enough, the weather got ugly and I marched over to his sales office.

"Hey," he greeted me.

"Where's my air conditioner?" I fumed.

"Well. ..."

"What part didn't you understand? The part where I was serious? Well, guess what. I'm going after your building license. Do you hear me now? We've been slapped around for six months, and I'm done with you. I'm contacting the state and requesting a hold on your license. You're not a builder and you shouldn't be in the business." My voice was low. Denny looked really uncomfortable. "Believe me, man. I'm going back to my house to begin the process."

Needless to say, a compressor was installed the very next day. The remainder of my punch list was whittled away, too. Don sent faxes from around the world to back me up, so everyone knew that Mr. and Mrs. Topping were on the same page.

—

It was impossible for me to enjoy our new house. Tradesmen would show up at the door wanting to be paid. I felt bad about this because we had paid the money to the builder. The marble foyer cracked that first winter, and we fought for warranty work. It was impossible to accept a compliment for our "dump".

One evening Barb, Mark, and Danny joined us for dinner in our home. Danny lay on the living room couch and was fed through a feeding tube. He was eight years old. It was cruel to see how life was treating him. While Barb and I moved to the kitchen to put the finishing touches on dinner, Gib stood next to Danny for a long time. The scene touched Barb and me. Gibby loved Danny.

Soon Gib ran into the kitchen to see Barb.

"Barb! You don't have to worry about Danny. God is talking to Danny," he announced.

"Oh I hope so, Sweetie. I sure hope so," she said. Barb just looked at me.

"I know. You don't have to say it," I said. It was a moving moment.

—

As part of my continuing education, I put together a home party with my psychic friend Elaine. When she entered the house, Gibby greeted her. "Hey! You're going on a 747 jet soon."

"Why, yes, I am," she laughed. She crouched down to be eye level with him while they talked about her upcoming flight to Alaska. I scurried about trying to make last- minute adjustments for my party.

"That's a very special boy you have there," she told me later.

"Yeah, tell me about it," I said, thinking about his learning difficulties, attention deficit disorder, and lack of patience. I was a little tired of all the 'specialness'.

"No, really. You have no idea how special he is. He's here to help the rest of us."

"Well, I'd like to see that! Hopefully he can help himself, too," I said.

"You know, your other son is here to help Gibby ground himself," she added.

I wasn't convinced, but I had to acknowledge that Nat's role in helping Gib during his early childhood was a key part of Gib's development.

Elaine laughed. "I see them as monks together in the 15th century. In Italy! They've had many lifetimes together."

I was intrigued. I could recall every detail of Gibby's infatuation with the huge crucifix hanging in the art museum the day we went to the Diego Rivera exhibit. He didn't respond to any other item of interest in the museum, but he threw a tantrum at leaving the 15th century Italian exhibit. I was also amazed at the depth of his fixation with the altar in the Lugano cathedral.

Elaine kept peering out my bedroom window with an intense scrutiny. "It's funny, but I keep seeing human bones in your yard. Whatever does that mean?"

I was horrified. "Oh, my gosh. I recently learned through neighborhood gossip that this area is reputed to have been an Indian burial ground. I'm not sure what that means, but I feel guilty having built a house here."

She continued to peer out the window. "It's all right. They are happy with your presence because they know you do not intend any disrespect. You appreciate nature."

I was greatly relieved, confused, amazed, and dubious. My thoughts rambled around in my brain in no particular order. Her words about loving nature struck me, since I was known for hugging my trees and patting the boulders affectionately. Imagining the boys as monks in Italy wasn't tough, either. There were so many coincidences in that possibility, as well. I was overloaded with coincidences, and I wasn't making any connections.

—

That summer we traveled to St. Louis for family time with Dad. If anything good could come from cancer, it would be the time allowed for closure. Don and his father had long talks about their relationship. Dad talked with the boys and held his granddaughter. As weak as he was from the ravages of the disease, he could not kick the nicotine addiction.

"Grandpa, please. Don't smoke. It's killing you," the boys would beg.

"I can't quit. I've tried, but I just can't," he'd say. "Promise me you will never, never start smoking."

The boys just stood before him, touched by what he was saying to them. They knew that he loved them so much he couldn't bear to consider them suffering the same fate. They nodded their little heads and promised him.

One afternoon Don and I crept out onto the cabin's deck to dash down to the lake for a swim. Dad was sleeping in his chair. I stopped dead in my tracks.

"Don," I whispered. "Aunt Ginny is here with Dad."

"What?" Don was puzzled; his aunt had died of cancer several years before.

"I can't see her, but I feel very strongly that she's visiting Dad right now. She's comforting him." I was as puzzled as Don because I'd never felt anything like it before. What an imagination I seemed to have.

Later, after his nap, Dad awoke really groggy and made his way into the house. "I know this sounds crazy," he announced to everyone present, "but I had the most vivid dream. My sister was here with me." He sat by himself for the longest time, lost in thought and puzzlement.

Don just looked at me. "How did you know?" he asked.

"Gosh, Hon, I don't know how. I just knew."

October came, and Don flew home every weekend as Dad's time drew near. The kids and I were too much disruption for that sensitive time and stayed home. On the first weekend of November, we were hosting a couple's shower for my sister's first baby, and Don reluctantly stayed home from St. Louis to help me. He was feeling guilty about not spending enough time with our children. An hour before the party was to start, we got the call that Dad had passed away. Personally, I felt he fought dying when he knew Don was going to be there for a visit. It was too late to cancel the party, so Don went for a long drive to be alone, and I entertained our guests. When the party ended, I hurriedly packed our clothes so we could leave for St. Louis.

When Gibby first saw Grandpa in his casket, he fled the room sobbing. I followed him outside and found him sitting at the driveway's curb with his head in his hands, just thinking. In that moment he seemed much older than his nine years.

"Hey. You okay?" I said as I sat next to him. I had expected to see him crying his heart out and was surprised at his calmness.

"Grandpa just said, 'Don't cry, Gibby. I'm OK.'"

"Grandpa? He's not here."

"I heard him in my head." Gib looked at me directly. It was important to him that I understand this. "I just heard him say, 'Don't cry, Gibby. I'm OK.'" I hugged him tightly. He and Grandpa had a special bond. Grandpa had always hurt over Gibby's struggles.

"Well, let's go back in and find Daddy, all right? You don't have to look in the casket if you don't want to. You know that's not Grandpa anymore. Grandpa's soul is freed from his sick body, and he's happy in heaven now." I pulled him to his feet.

"It's OK, Mom. He said not to cry, and I won't." I never saw him shed another tear.

In March, all three of our children took turns with bouts of chickenpox, not at the same time, but at two-week intervals. It was excruciating for me. Don was out of the country on business, and I couldn't take a break to drive to the grocery store. My friends were helpful, dropping supplies off at the front door, and I nursed each child when it was his or her turn.

Barb popped in one afternoon while Gib was convalescing. She and Mark were buying a new home, and as she drew the floor plan, it became apparent to me that Danny would never live there. I sat back in my chair with the shock of my insight. Within minutes Gib came down the hallway from where he was watching television.

"Barb!" he said, as he maneuvered next to her for his customary hug. "Why does Danny have to die?"

"Well, Sweetie," Barb said sadly. "His body is broken and he's very sick. He isn't going to live as long as you or me." Oh my gosh, I thought. He knows, too.

"But why does he have to die now?" he objected.

"We don't know how much time he has, honey," Barb answered, looking puzzled.

"Gibby, God will take care of Danny. Don't you worry," I said. After thinking about it for a minute, he decided to return to the television and ran off.

Danny died the following week.

CHAPTER NINE

Death is not extinguishing the light; it is only putting out
the lamp because the dawn has come.
Rabindranath Tagore

The boys went to the funeral home with me, but I went alone to the
funeral. I had a dream the night before in which Danny stood before
a bright white light. He extended his arms to be enfolded into the
light, welcoming him home. I was stunned by how real the dream
seemed, and I knew he was relieved to be free of his task and safely
"home" again.

The funeral was painfully hard. We all were relieved to have
him finished with his hideous suffering, but looking at that small
casket at the front of the church and singing "Jesus Loves the Little
Children" was too much to bear.

I was conflicted with emotion: grief that his path had been so
difficult; gratitude that he led us to Switzerland; grief that he hadn't
been helped; gratitude that Gib had; grief for Barb and Mark's loss;
gratitude that they loved him so completely. *Please God*, I prayed
fervently, *don't let his suffering have been for nothing.*

In later years, Barb learned that marijuana grown in Hawaii
had high mercury content from volcanic soils. Dan's birth mother
had been a user, which could explain the content in his liver. There
was some question over mercury being used in disposable diapers.
Also, there was quite a controversy concerning the use of mercury
as a preservative in vaccinations that was believed to be causing

grave illnesses in children during a certain time frame. Dan's first vaccinations had been followed by convulsions. Hopefully, people in a position to make a difference looked at the history and symptoms of children like Danny, did the math, and put an end to this practice.

Barb was relieved by the explanation these revelations provided, but nothing could counterbalance the fact that their reputations had been trashed in the legal proceedings. Or that confidential information had been treated so callously.

I was grateful. I can't begin to describe how it felt to have my life back in control. Gib's illness had been like a vortex sucking me down into an abyss. To have him stronger, happier, healthier, and moving forward was a joy I can't describe.

Barb was generous. "It is such a gift to have him healing," she would say, and I marveled at her emotional maturity. If she ever felt envy or sadness in comparing her situation to mine, I never saw any evidence of it. She was all about love, and I know that she made God proud.

I was raising the children Catholic, as I'd promised in my marriage vows. We had a combined Lutheran and Catholic ceremony, and although I'd promised to raise them Catholic, I'd warned the priest that they'd be getting a Protestant perspective on religion. The priest laughed when I told him that and said he thought that was just great. I had since learned that the doctrines were so similar, I wasn't having any problem adjusting.

I found old-school Catholics were having a harder time that I was. I'd tried taking classes to convert, but this environment also handled others having problems within the faith as well as some uber-Catholics who felt they were the only true church. The priest handling the instruction was wonderful, but I felt overwhelmed by all the agendas being addressed. With so much confusion, how could I possible join?

I was diligent about evening prayers with the kids because I wanted them to forge a personal connection with God. I love a common prayer that unites everyone's soul and intention; the spiritual connection is awesome. I also wanted our kids to have a friendship with Him. I encouraged them to tell Him about their day and ask Him to protect them.

They were cute.

"Hi, God. I had a good day today," they'd begin. Then they'd share some of their highlights. "I got a good grade on my science test. Nessa made me mad and I hit her, but I'm sorry. I gave her a hug and will never do it again. Mom was mad at me. Please protect me while I'm sleeping. See you tomorrow! Amen."

I wanted them to trust that God would protect them. I would often tell them, "If you ever have a nightmare, you just say, 'You can't have me. I'm a child of God's,' and you will be safe. You were baptized. You're God's little child." It must have been a good strategy, because they never once awakened me due to having a nightmare.

Going to church was fun. After one Mass, the fellowship committee served donuts and coffee for a social opportunity.

"OK! Hurray! We're going to God's house. We're going to say 'Hi,' then have some donuts!" the kids would sing on the way to church.

One night I was restless and sleeping fitfully. I opened my eyes and saw the image of three people climbing through our bedroom window. They walked through the bedroom and disappeared out the door.

I sat straight up. "Don." I smacked his rump. "Wake up! Somebody was just in here."

"What?" he bounded out of bed half asleep. "Where?"

"They were like ghosts or something. They climbed through the window and walked through."

"You mean they weren't real? You were dreaming?" he gasped, trying to follow my story. He climbed back into bed.

"I'm sorry. I've never had anything like this happen before. It was real." My heart was pounding. "I feel violated." It took a long time for me to calm down.

The next morning, as I dropped Vanessa off at her preschool, I learned that her classroom had been broken into and items had been stolen.

"This is weird. I dreamt about this last night," I said.

"How many were there?" the owner asked me.

"Three. Two boys and a girl. They were teenagers."

She nodded her head. "We knew there had to be more than two" was all she said. I was amazed that she didn't question the method through which the information came.

I was getting very caught up with fundraising for the school. I wanted the kids to have it all: a good library, computer laboratory, playground, science equipment and art supplies. I started a Cub Scout pack because I'd read articles about childhood self-esteem that cited the Boy Scout program as the best source. Another mother and I started a hot lunch program, and a few of us organized a PTO.

I threw myself into service. I was so full of gratitude I thought my heart would burst. I couldn't possibly pay back the grace we had been given.

These were such busy years for me. I realized that my management degree had prepared me for the chaos of tracking the intimate details for five of us. At last, I felt prepared for my job. Motivating the children required finesse, and keeping their dad an integral part of our lives while he traveled was especially challenging. I filled every parental role in Don's absence, struggling to keep balance in our lives. Don wasn't with them enough to handle discipline without their resentment, but I certainly made sure they understood respect for their father.

I knew being the sole disciplinarian would be risky, but I had a full day to love them. I would be the target for their frustrations, and I knew I would be making mistakes as well without having the benefit of a second opinion. I encouraged them to speak their minds, in a respectful manner, to insure they had a voice. I consulted parenting articles for single parents so I didn't over-mother our sons and create future situations for rebellion. I simply did the best I could under the circumstances.

Don's job placed social responsibilities on me that provided interesting experiences. I volunteered with the clients' charities and attended dinner functions. This was sometimes challenging. I'd spend my day driving kids and handling last- minute illnesses and other assorted crises. Then I'd race to the bedroom to transform into black tie attire and scoot out the door before baby Nessie could smear me with viscous matter. My brain would switch to grown-up mode while I fought the urge to cut up the food on people's plates before they ate.

My grandmother was failing miserably, and it broke my heart. One afternoon I entered her room at the nursing home and saw that she was working intently on something. I approached her and realized that her wrists were tied to the arms of her wheelchair. I knew this was for her safety, since she'd been trying to get up and walk on her own while being too weak to do so safely, but it was horrifying to think of having her hands restrained. She held a plastic knife from her lunch tray and tried to cut the restraints off.

"Grandma. What are you doing?"

She looked at me soulfully. "I've got to get out of here." I felt dreadful for not helping her escape, but she really needed nursing care to rehabilitate.

I visited weekly to take her for walks in her wheelchair outdoors and to social activities within the home. Mom visited weekly as well. We wanted the staff to know that this old woman was loved and cared for and should not be overlooked.

The staph infection she'd caught in the hospital when she'd had her broken hip would not go away and eventually wore her down. Grandma was admitted to the hospital and lapsed into a coma. Mom and I were alternating our visiting days to insure constant interaction.

One afternoon I had the impulse to take my Bible along. I read the Bible, but I'm terrible at memorizing it. Truth be known, I was always creeped out by people who boastfully quoted it verse and chapter. I don't think it's respectful of God for us to be so prideful. For me, faith is personal and intimate. Here I was now, holding my Bible and not sure what I wanted to do with it except I knew without doubt that my grandma loved the Lord. I'd read that coma patients could hear, so I said a quick prayer asking God to guide me. When I opened the Bible, I started reading. Coincidentally, it was about "going home." I didn't think this would sound comforting to my feisty grandma lying there in a coma, but I'd asked for guidance, so I stuck with it.

Soon it was time for me to leave and pick up the kids from school.

"Grandma, I need to leave." I spoke to her as though she were conscious. "I need to hurry before school lets out. I'll come in tomorrow and read more of the Bible if you'd like." I packed my book bag and turned to kiss her goodbye. I was stunned. She was looking at me, moving her mouth and trying to tell me something. I put my head close to hers to hear better, but she was too weak. Still, I was surprised that she was awake and trying to interact.

I stroked her little gray head. "I love you, Grandma. I'm sorry you're so sick. I wish I could take it away for you." Her mouth kept working, and I stayed until she stopped trying to communicate.

"I'll see you tomorrow. I love you." I kissed her forehead. She closed her eyes when I left, but I could see pain and discomfort on her face. She passed away that evening. My other mother went home, the one who was never angry with me, who patiently taught me to knit and crochet, helped me sew, encouraged me to breast-feed my babies, taught me gardening, listened to my woes and shared her stories. It was a huge loss for me.

—

Gibby's problems at school and with life continued to bat me around like an old rolled-up sock. He was so frustrated. He was an easy target for the taunts of other children. His school was a safe haven, but everywhere else was a reminder that he wasn't able to defend himself physically or verbally. I kept a close eye on him and kept him from as much as I could.

Fourth grade was a nightmare. It's just something about the age, I think. One of Gib's friends — I'll call him Gary — was an absolute darling when he was six, but this year he was a different person. The torment kept our household on an emotional roller coaster, but then came the day when Gary invited Gib over to play.

It was their first playdate that school year. Gib was thrilled that his old best friend had returned from craziness. I let Gib go on a day I was preparing for a dinner party we were hosting. Gib was returned home earlier than I expected, and as I opened the door, Gib shot past me up the stairs. I greeted Gary, who walked Gib to the door, and was vaguely puzzled by the look on Gary's face. Well, maybe the boys didn't end their day on an up note; it happens.

Our guests arrived, we enjoyed a lively dinner in the dining room, and I excused myself to prepare the desserts. Gib came into the kitchen and was quite agitated. "Mom," he cried, "You've got to do something about Gary. He shot me in the back with a rifle, and it hurt a lot."

"What? Gary shot you with a rifle?"

"Yes he did, and it hurt!" Gib cried.

"I didn't know he played with guns." I reached over to him quickly to check him over. This was bothersome because I thought I knew the parents and would never have guessed this latest development. Gib had played over there many times over the years, and I was amazed at the change in values between us. Oh well, I guess we won't be playing over there again any time soon, I mused.

"That's not all!" Gib cried. "When we were in the woods, Gary pulled a knife on me and told me to take my clothes off!"

I was stunned. A knife, too? What the hell was going on over there?

"Gib. Are you sure he pulled a knife on you and threatened you?"

"Yes, Mom. He told me to take my clothes off and he pointed a big knife at me."

"Sweetie, what did you do?" I croaked.

"I took my jacket off, then I took my shirt off, then I got cold, then I got really mad and started screaming at him. I grabbed my clothes and ran back to his house. I told them I wanted to go home. I wanted to call my Mom now!" He was practically dancing around the kitchen with agitation.

"Did you tell them what happened?" I was just stunned.

"No, Gary begged me to forgive him. He said he was sorry, don't tell his Dad, please. He seemed really, really scared. He begged me not to tell. But I made them bring me home," Gib wailed.

"OK, Sweetie, don't worry. You're safe now. I will take care of it." I hugged him and with his heart unburdened, he scampered upstairs.

From where I stood in the kitchen, the world seemed to stop. I remembered my jovial guests, called Don into the kitchen and shared briefly the events of Gib's day. I gave Don quick instructions for completing the dessert and coffee, grabbed the phone and retreated into the relative silence of the laundry room so that I could have a conversation with Gary's father.

"Hi Sue, what's up?" Gary's father greeted me. He was a great guy and I always enjoyed talking with him.

"Listen, Gib just came home with a wild story about Gary shooting him in the back with a rifle."

"Wow," he said. "I figured they had a fight of some kind when Gib demanded to go home, but Gary said he didn't know why Gib was so upset. They were playing with Gary's air rifle, but Gary knows how to use that responsibly; that thing takes the heads off squirrels at 50 feet."

"You mean you let your son play with air rifles?" I croaked into the phone. I couldn't believe I was hearing this.

"It just shoots BBs. I was very thorough with gun safety when we gave the gun to him," he said.

"You don't think a 9-year-old might suffer a lack of judgment while playing with an air rifle powerful enough to take the head off a squirrel at 50 feet?" My voice was starting to escalate. "Fine, but my biggest concern is for his pulling a knife on Gib and demanding he strip. This is an act of degradation, and I really want an answer for it. I have dinner guests I need to return to, but I'd really like an answer for what the hell went on over there today. I'll call you tomorrow around noon for an explanation." We concluded our conversation and I hung up the phone.

The next morning I called Gary's father for the full story.

"Well, here's the deal, Sue," he began. "I talked with Gary about this, and he has no idea why Gib would make up such an awful story."

I paused. "So this is a case of your kid's word against my kid?" I asked.

"Well, basically yes," he agreed.

"You've know Gib a long time. You know he's language-impaired and has a hard time communicating his thoughts and emotions. Lying does not even occur to him, but I hear what you are saying." My mind was quickly calculating the teasing and taunting Gib would suffer at the hands of Gary at school over this. "Let me make sure you understand this," I said. "There will be no repercussions from this on Gib at school, or I will call the police. I will also give a heads up to the staff for the potential of problems from this so that they will be on the lookout for Gib's well-being."

I hung up the phone fuming, promising myself to find a psychologist to help Gib with victimhood issues. I just knew this beloved friend turning on him would lead to a host of issues, and boy, it sure did. That psychologist was on our payroll for quite a few years.

Even though Gib looked normal, kids just seem to have a sense of someone being different or feeling insecure. We would be at the ski lodge with his ski club and I'd notice other children, complete strangers, eyeing him and snickering. Catechism was a nightmare, too. Anywhere he was on his own became a cattle call for bullies, and it drove me crazy. It was hard on Nathaniel, too, since he usually shared a classroom with Gibby. Other classmates would make comments like, "I can't believe you're related to him." Nat was usually in a state of frustration. He dropped several friends over their attitudes about his brother.

When they'd share their day with me, I'd feel like a nut case. Gib would wail, "I only got 56 percent on my science test." I'd say, "Well, what did you get on the last one?" He'd answer, "46 percent." I would compliment him, saying, "Wow, that's great. You improved."

Then Nat would say "Hey Mom, I got 87 percent on the science test." I'd respond by asking what his previous score had been. When he said, "Oh, I think it was 97 percent," I'd answer, "Really? Do you think you did your personal best?" Nat would be so frustrated, but

I cheered when they bested their last score because I wanted them to compare their performance to themselves. That was all they had control of. Competing against others could really lead to self-esteem issues.

One night, as I climbed the stairs to check on the kids before retiring for the night, I heard sobbing from the boys' room. I discovered that Gib was the source. He was in the corner of his room, sitting on the floor and crying his eyes out. I sat next to him and gathered him onto my lap. "What's wrong, Sweetie?"

"I just want to know why Nat is so smart and I'm so stupid," he wailed. Nat was sleeping in the next bed, oblivious to all of this, and I felt my heart rip in two. As careful as I'd always been never to compare the two boys, it hadn't entirely mattered. Gib wasn't stupid. He knew the difference, and he didn't understand it.

"Oh, Gibby. What makes you think he's so smart?"

"Everyone thinks so. Everyone likes him better. He gets good grades, and I'm the dummy."

This was one of the lowest moments in my life. I held him until he stopped crying, thankful that I'd found him in this moment.

"Well, let me tell you. I love you. Daddy loves you. Nat and Nessie love you. Your grandmas and grandpas love you. Jesus loves you, and God loves you. Do you think it matters to any of us who is smarter? Huh? Has there ever been a contest? No. And let me tell you, Nat's not always so smart. How many jackets has he lost? Three. How many times do I have to remind him to go back into the bathroom and brush his teeth?"

Gib started to giggle.

"Sweetie, we are all unique with our own specialness. It doesn't matter what other people are doing; we all have our personal job to do in life. You're my only Gibby, and you don't need to compare yourself to anyone. Just do your personal best. Now hop into bed." I tucked him in and kissed him before turning out the light.

When I fell into my own bed, I started to cry. In my care not to compare the kids to each other, I'd failed to realize that it didn't totally matter. They would compare themselves. This poor kid had been through so much; when was it going to stop? Now he was devaluing himself. And where was Don when I needed him? In Australia, of course, traveling on business. Why was I always alone for these things?

When I'd had enough of my pity party, I thought about my emotional state. *Well, if I were ever going to go out of body, this would be the night for it. I'm so emotional,* I said to myself. I prayed my usual bedtime prayers, asking for guidance, blessing, and protection for us all.

The next morning I entered the boys' room to get them ready for school. Nat sat straight up in bed and looked at me suspiciously.

"I want to know why you were in our room last night looking like a ghost," he demanded.

"What?" I laughed. "Oh, no, Honey. I was sitting on the floor with Gib. We were talking for a while before going to bed."

"No, you weren't. Gib was asleep," he accused. "You came in the room, looked at us and walked across the room into the closet. Just like a ghost," he insisted.

"What do you know about ghosts?" I teased. "You must have been dreaming."

"I know what I saw, Mom," he stated with frustration.

"Well, I don't know, but you need to get up and get dressed. We don't want to be late for school." I thought to myself that I must have gone out of body to double-check on them during the night. The next couple of days I'd catch Nat eyeing me suspiciously.

I had so many unexplained spiritual things occurring during those years.

One night I woke for no apparent reason and saw an orb of gold and silver light by my bed. It was sparkling and beautiful. I watched it for the longest time before going back to sleep. I never knew what it was.

Another time I was awakened by a pressure on top of my body. I felt like I was being squeezed. Thankfully, Don was home, because I bolted upright in a panic.

"Don! Someone was here, squeezing me." I was clearly frightened.

"Who?" Don was real groggy.

"I don't know who."

"What popped into your mind?"

"Nothing! I was just sleeping. It was as though its face covered mine, and it was squeezing." I was really upset.

Don swooped his arm around me and pulled me against his chest. I tried to quiet my mind, so I could return to sleep.

"But I've never felt attacked before," I whispered to him.

"It's okay, Hon. Just say a prayer for protection," Don murmured. I was awake a long time that night.

The next morning my sister called, worried and upset. "Have you been to a doctor for a checkup recently?" she fussed.

I yawned. "What? Yes, of course. I get yearly physicals."

"I had a dream about you last night, and you were dead."

"What? Why don't you explain the dream to me? It probably means something else," I laughed.

"It's not funny; it was real. I had two people behind me, encouraging me to approach this woman who had her back toward me. She was your height and build, and I didn't want to go to you because I knew it was you, and you were dead." She practically sobbed. "They kept urging me, moving me toward you. When I finally got the nerve to grab your shoulder and turn you, I was horrified that it was you. I didn't want you to be dead. I grabbed you and hugged you to me as tightly as I could because I didn't want to let you go."

"That was YOU in my room last night!" I shouted into the phone.

"What are you talking about?"

"It was you squeezing and suffocating me. Holy cow, you scared the crap out of me," I yelled. I was so excited.

"What are you talking about? I don't understand any of this."

I quickly related the events of the night before.

"What does it mean, then?" she insisted.

"It means that I wasn't dead; I was out of body," I explained. "We often do that when sleeping. You were out, too. Your guides were trying to teach you that our souls live eternally; they don't die. Sometimes at night we're learning lessons. They wanted to prove to you that you don't need to be afraid. Our souls live. Damn, girl. You scared me half to death. I could feel your head in my face."

"This is so weird," my sister said. We talked for an hour about metaphysical phenomena.

When we told Mom, she said, "You know, there are a lot of nights when I can't sleep and I'm up in my living room. You two just stay away from me, you hear?" We laughed hard with her.

I was also having vivid pictures pop into my head at random times, like when I was driving the car, washing the dishes, or taking a shower. I kept seeing a small white bungalow with a big shade tree to the right of the house and a cornfield behind it. A young woman stood to the left of the house, in the shade of the big tree and wearing a full apron.

I guess I'd been shown this picture one too many times, because I mentioned to my mother that I was losing my mind.

"Tell me about it," she encouraged me one day. When I finished, she said, "That sounds like the house where I was born in New Goshen, Indiana. New Goshen is where Grandpa worked in the coal mines until my parents decided to move to Michigan for an electrician job at Fisher Body. The mining company owned the town's only store, so my dad always complained that the company was the first to get his wages back. The mine had been a risky employment source for impoverished families. They lived in dread of the whistle blowing during the middle of the day. It meant a cave-in," she reminisced. "You should stop there sometime on your drive to St. Louis."

We looked it up on the atlas, and I laughed that Don would never deviate from the freeway. Our visit time with his relatives was too short as it was, without wasting time on this side trip.

"Heck, let's just take a trip down there and I'll show you myself," Mom said. We made plans for the kids and me to ride in my parents' van with them.

I recognized the house from my dream the minute I saw it. I asked Dad to stop in front of the house, and I devoured every detail with my eyes. I recognized the coolness of the huge shade tree, the bright sunlit cornfield behind the house, and the small white bungalow.

The only detail missing was my grandmother, but I understood instantly what she wanted me to know. When she'd been alive, she'd had an unhealthy love for her material belongings. Her stuff, for that was what it meant to me, often appeared to mean more to her than we did. So many visits were met with, "Take your shoes off before coming into the house," rather than, "I'm so glad you came to visit me." Or she'd say, "Sit on that chair carefully," instead of, "Oh, just sit anywhere." On a rainy day, she would call us to pick her up to run her errands rather than drive her clean car in that mess. It really drove us crazy.

Now, as I looked at this humble home, I understood that her possessions were important to her because they had been so hard to obtain. Suddenly, my memory replayed her saying, "It doesn't matter how poor you are. There is no excuse for not having clean, mended curtains." I knew that, at one time, her pride was all she'd owned. They were poor, they worked hard, they were good people, and they built a life for themselves. It was humbling, and I knew it was important for her to have me understand this.

I felt thoughtful for the remainder of the day, speechless that I'd seen this place in my mind, that it persisted enough for me to travel here and learn something about my grandmother's character. There were too many coincidences in my life. What was coincidence, anyway? Was it mankind's way to rationalize spiritual intervention?

We stayed in a hotel with six floors and took adjoining rooms on the top floor. This was a concern for my mother because her knees were in bad shape. She usually insisted on the first or second floor so that she could handle the stairs in an emergency. We didn't have reservations, so we couldn't be particular about the rooms that were available for us, but the sixth floor was a worry. We settled in for an evening of television while Dad snoozed on his bed, exhausted from a full day of driving us around. At one point I thought I heard an alarm ringing and jumped up to open our door to the hallway. There was silence. Mom and the kids eyed me suspiciously.

"What was that?" I paced to the window to look out.

"What?" Mom asked.

"That alarm. Where was it coming from? Did you hear it?"

"There wasn't any alarm," Mom responded.

"Sure there was. I clearly heard it. It wasn't in the hall. Was it on television?" I insisted.

"No." Everyone looked at me in amazement.

"Hm. That's crazy." I dismissed it.

That night I had a tough time sleeping. The boys were in the bed next to me, while Nessie shared a bed with me. She was awfully restless, kicking me in the side and rolling into me. *Man,* I thought to myself, *If I don't get some sleep I will never have the patience to handle them tomorrow.* I repositioned Nessie, and then rolled over to face the room.

I was stunned to see a white shadowy column of light between myself and the television set. It stood about five feet tall, didn't move and didn't make a sound. I squinted my eyes, and then opened them to reassess the situation. Was this a ghost?

I was intrigued. My mind was blank because I was curious, and I understood that I shouldn't be afraid. I sure didn't want to get out of bed and walk by it, but I was impressed that I felt so calm. I believed it wanted me to understand that I should not be afraid, that everything would be all right. In fact, that was the only thought I held while watching this curious white shadow. Maybe it was Grandma; the day had been about her, after all.

After a long while, I puzzled why it hadn't left me. Finally, I decided to roll over and face the wall. Surely it would leave then. When I glanced back to see if I had been successful, I saw it was still there. I turned back to the wall, waited a bit, and then looked over my shoulder again. It still hadn't left. I started to feel uncomfortable. I faced the wall again and struggled to talk my way out of fearfulness, eventually dozing to sleep. The last time I looked, the apparition had left. Then I went to sleep.

About 3 a.m., I was awakened by fire alarms. I sat up with a start, remembering the apparition and the alarms I'd heard earlier in the evening. My mother flew into our room to help me get the

113

kids up. I was worried about the stairwell and her knees, and she was in a panic.

"Mom," I said calmly, "it's OK. Ask Dad to call the desk to double check." She looked at me like I'd lost my mind, so I tried another approach.

"Dad," I called out as I stuck my head into their room. "Call the desk to see if this is a false alarm." Dad nodded and reached for the phone. As he hung up the phone, he announced that it was indeed a false alarm; it was an equipment problem. The noise soon abated, and we put the children back into their beds.

"How did you know?" Mom whispered.

"Something spiritual was here. I think it may have been Grandma, telling me not to be afraid, that it would be all right." I quickly explained what I'd experienced. Mom looked dumbfounded. When she turned toward her room, she tossed back,

"You're one crazy lady, you know that? I'll see you in the morning."

Slowly, I was feeling a major shift in my belief system. It didn't matter to me whether others believed me. I knew my own reality and would never view my life the same way after that trip.

CHAPTER TEN

Don't believe what your eyes are telling you. All they show
is limitation. Look with your understanding, find out
what you already know, and you'll see the way to fly.

Richard Bach

I was still trying to process Gibby's unique skills. One night he
accosted one of our dinner guests and told him not to take the
white plane with the blue letters. Gib adored "Captain Phil" and
was insistent about the flight.

Phil said, "Oh, don't worry. I know what you're talking about.
Continental has white planes. I'm taking a Northwest flight, and
those planes are silver with red, white, and blue markings."

Gib was not reassured. "No. It's a white plane with blue letters.
Don't take it."

"Gibby, I'm taking a Northwest flight in the morning." He
picked Gib up into his arms and flew him around the living room.
Gib laughed with delight, but when Phil left our home, Gibby
reminded him.

"OK, OK. I promise I will not take the white plane with the blue
letters." Phil left our house laughing with us about this wackiness.

We heard later that his plane had technical difficulties, but
the same flight to South America was available on Continental if
customers wanted to switch over. Phil said he didn't take the flight.
He never heard whether anything happened to that flight, but if Gib
knew that much, he decided he wouldn't mess with the rest of it.

One morning while I was driving the kids to school, Gib announced, "Mom! I'm worried about Dad in the big city. There's danger there!"

Speech was not something that came easily for Gibby, so when his language was clear and concise, I paid attention.

"Well, yes, Daddy's in New York City today. I'll warn him when he calls us tonight," I said.

"There is danger there! There's a bad man. You've got to warn him."

"Yes, honey, I will. When Daddy calls me tonight, I will tell him what you said." I was trying to calm him down, but I was a little spooked.

When Don called home that night, I said, "For what it's worth, Gibby's worried about your safety in the big city." I repeated the warning. "Just a heads up, okay? Be extra careful."

"Weird. OK, sure," Don agreed.

The next morning, while I was again driving the children to school, Gib repeated his warning. "Mom! There's danger. Did you tell Dad?"

"Yes, Sweetie, I told him last night when he called. He promised to be extra careful," I reassured. "He'll be home tonight, OK?" Gib nodded his head in agreement.

When Don returned home that night, I said, "So, what happened today?"

"Oh my God, you won't believe it. I was just exiting the Helmsley Hotel to walk to the office when I noticed a movement out of the corner of my eye. I just instinctively stepped back into the doorframe, narrowly avoiding a collision with a man running down the sidewalk. The policemen were pursuing him, and their guns were drawn. The suspect ran up and over cars to escape, like something out of a cop show. The weirdest thing ever, he was wearing a sweatshirt that said, "Michigan." Isn't that a riot? What a coincidence." He laughed.

In the next moment he was addressing me soberly. "If I hadn't been alert, that dude would have careened right into me and sent me flying. I have no doubt I would have been injured." Don looked at me thoughtfully. "How does he know these things?"

"He's special," I grinned. I was so used to his "specialness" causing Gibby so many problems in his life that I was grateful it was such a blessing in this instance.

During his years in lower elementary school I became aware of a theory concerning spiritually enlightened youngsters called Blue Indigo Children. A researcher using Kirlian photography to see the human aura noticed that certain children had a deep blue, indigo-colored field. Attributes these kids often share include attention deficit disorder or attention deficit hyperactive disorder. They tend to be headstrong, empathetic, or intuitive, and they possess a deep desire to help the world. They frequently present themselves as frail, or with allergies.

I was fascinated because the attributes certainly pertained to Gibby. I read "The Indigo Children", by Tober and Carroll, that suggested these children were at a new stage of evolution rather than the medical diagnoses often diagnosed. I read up on this phenomenon, but since it was a new concept and there wasn't any answer regarding what I could do to make him fit into life better, I filed the information away in my mind. As I moved forward with raising Gib, it helped to know there were other children that fit the description of Indigo Children. His spiritual awareness was certainly a skill not to be ignored.

I continued keeping the children God-loving. We talked with Him daily, which was what I called our prayers. Because we attended a private secular school, we took religious instruction at the church. Those class times could get rowdy, as children were expected to attend another hour of class time after a full school day. The classmates were from the public schools, didn't know us at all, and saw our sons as easy prey.

The final straw was the year Nat and Gib were in confirmation. Gib was tormented mercilessly. I would always ask the teacher not to ask him an open-ended question because he was speech-impaired, but they'd forget.

"Hey, Retard," the kids would whisper behind the teacher's back. "Hey, Stupid. What are you, retarded or something?"

Finally Nat could bear no more. "Leave him alone."

"Mind your own business. Do you want me to beat you up?" was the response.

"I am minding my own business. He's my brother, and I suggest you remember where you are right now and start acting like a Christian," Nat retorted.

When I picked them up, they were both wailing. Gib was hurt and offended. Nat was freaked by the hypocrisy of the situation, and Nessie was indignant that the boys in her class were so sassy to the volunteer who was teaching. I pulled them out of religious education, explaining to the staff that it was important that church be a place of refuge for them, not a source of conflict. Rather than skew their opinion of church, I would teach them at home. The staff understood. They were apologetic and generous about sharing their materials with me.

"If that's what Catholics do, I don't want to be any part of them," the boys insisted.

"Guys, it's not Catholics. It's children being bad, that's all. Wait until you're older and you see grown-ups being bad. That's really awful. We are going to continue worshipping at our church, and we're going to continue being nice to people," I said.

Things at school were turning sour as well. Nat and Gib were in a split class, and as classmates struggled with hormone rages, Gib became one of the prey. To make matters worse, Nat's chums joined in the targeting. Nat was wounded deeply that the kids he counted as buddies could tear into his brother. Nat defended his brother, was hurt over the lack of respect his friends had for him, and slowly disengaged from those friends.

As much as he understood the situation, he also couldn't help resenting the stress Gib caused him. It was heartbreaking to process this side of human nature with him, and those boys lost a loyal, fun friend in Nathaniel. Nat squared his shoulders and endured each day. I did my best and took them to a child psychologist to learn coping techniques. I hoped these experiences would be character building, rather than detrimental.

That summer, while on our family vacation, Gib moaned and cried continually. I'd been concerned about depression, since it ran in the family, and warranted that the circumstances of his life were enough to be depressed about. I had previously set up an appointment with a psychiatrist upon our return. For the time being we were trapped in the van with his misery as we headed toward the East Coast.

One day he announced, "I might as well kill myself. I'm damaged goods anyway."

"Sue?" Don said with alarm. "Are you hearing this?"

"Already on it. We've got an appointment with a psychiatrist when we return."

We then proceeded to process the crisis with Gib. No, he couldn't kill himself. He was a cherished, loved child of God with a purpose for being in this life. We promised him help when we returned home.

—

The psychological evaluation for Gib's high school program was a disaster. The testing was language-based and seemed designed to record failure for Gib. When the results were to be revealed, I drove to the clinic in Detroit, and Don met me there from work.

The doctor told us Gib's IQ was below normal. The rest of the blabbing was incoherent to me. Don had to lead me out of the clinic. Once on the street, I started to cry. Don steered me into the nearest restaurant, into the back booth for coffee.

"Don," I wept, "what has all this been for? He was developmentally disabled all along, and I couldn't accept that? Has this been about my ego, willing him to be something he's not capable of?" I didn't feel like I was giving up on him, like I had years before when God had chided me. I sincerely felt I was suffering a reality check. Maybe I'd been delusional.

"Stop it," Don admonished. "You know in your heart that's not true. That doctor is full of crap, do you hear me? Crap! We'll get another opinion."

"Why? To hear the same thing from another doctor? Their methods are all the same."

"No. I don't care how many opinions we need to get. Someone must be able to test intelligence fairly."

I remembered the original speech evaluation all those years ago, and how the tester had cautioned me never to believe what I was told about a low IQ. Developing his own sign language was an indicator of very high intelligence. I clung to that advice to save my sanity, but I was concerned that the high school of our choice wouldn't admit Gib.

Once again, I pestered the Lord with my problems.

"Lord, please guide me to where I need to be with your child," I prayed fervently.

I was never answered by a thundering voice on high. I was answered with quiet thoughts, insights, and ideas. I was given serendipitous moments, coincidences and little miracles. I would get the information I needed in unlikely ways. I needed to listen, and I needed to have the faith to act.

Shortly after I'd had the evaluation experience, a friend called. We hadn't spoken for a long time. She had two hyperactive sons and was involved in her school's support group.

"I just heard about a school psychologist who has a private practice for intelligence testing for special needs children," she said. "She was a speech pathologist early in her career. I couldn't help thinking of you."

It was just that simple.

The afternoon that Dr. Z. tested Gib was memorable for us. She came to our home, the most relaxing environment for Gib, and took the time to acquaint herself with him before administering the test.

"Here," she said to me. "Let me show you this test for language-impaired students." She spread the document before me and was quite excited about it.

"Each of these symbols represents a word," she explained as she showed me what looked like hieroglyphics. "Now look what happens when we combine symbols to tell a story."

I tried to read a sentence of symbols and lost the ability after four items. "Wow. This is impossible," I laughed.

"Really? Gib's score was off the charts. If you took his IQ from this test, it is in the highly superior range. Do you know what that means?" she said, emphatically. "This kid gets language, all right; it just isn't English."

"Yeah? Well, English seems to be what everyone is using these days," I said.

"Exactly. That's his disability. But his intelligence is superior." I sat back to digest this. I had certainly never heard this before.

"This is amazing," she continued. "Can you imagine most people judging you to be stupid, when in fact you're the one who is more intelligent? Because that is his reality." I considered the impact of this reality on Gib. How did this child get all the luck? I could not begin to fathom the depth of his frustration and despair.

The testing report put his IQ within the normal range, and we were admitted to the school of our choice.

When we picked a high school environment, we chose one of the best private schools for the learning disabled. Public school would have been sheer trauma. Gib lacked physicality, and his expressive problems prevented him from verbal defense. We now knew we had to deal with attention deficit disorder, dyslexia, language-expressive impairment, math disabilities, and depression.

I thought about the institution, a private school we'd considered for Gib's elementary education, and I was thankful that we hadn't chosen it then. Now it was a fresh environment for Gib, and he was thrilled to graduate from the eighth grade and enter high school. If he'd attended this school from kindergarten through 12th grade, he would have burned out. Here we were with a new school that provided a low student-teacher ratio and all the support we could ever want. The entire population was like Gib, and for the first time in his life he did not feel stupid. He was emotionally safe, and the staff's attention to his needs allowed him his first successes ever.

I expressed my gratitude in prayer and in service. I continued fundraising efforts for the schools as well as other nonprofits, and my heart sang its thanks to God for pulling me out of the abyss, as I'd taken to calling Gib's earlier years.

Don attended the first parent-teacher conference with me. He was facing a transfer to New York, and I was working hard with the educators to find a comparable solution on the East Coast. I could not find a school that offered everything Gib needed for his myriad disabilities that didn't require boarding. It horrified me to think of sending a child away to school during the formative years. The parent-teacher conference was wonderful. The teachers were thrilled with his progress, which was apparent to us as we lived with him.

When we left the school, Don turned to me and said, "I'm going to decline the transfer."

"What?" I couldn't believe it. We'd never discussed not going.

"How can I possibly interrupt Gib's progress? This is the first hopeful report we've ever had for him. I'm not about to ask him to give this up."

"But Don, you can't just turn it down. The chairman of the board specifically asked you to be on his team. What if he holds this against your career?" I said.

"Then so be it. Look, up until now you've been the one making all the sacrifices. I'm happy to take my turn." Don was quietly emphatic. His decision was made, and to my knowledge he's never regretted it.

Those were the best years to be Gib's parents. It was a reprieve. We were in the hands of caring, supportive, professional advocates for alternative learning. School was not about measuring his failure. It began to prepare him for life with coping techniques and methods for survival, impressing upon his fragile self-esteem that he could celebrate his uniqueness. The reprieve allowed me to put more focus on our other two children, and the joy in my heart resurrected my zany sense of humor.

When we considered high schools for Nathaniel, we wanted an environment that challenged him academically and enforced our value system. I was greatly relieved when he agreed to attend an all-male Catholic high school. Nat's high scores on the entrance exam resulted in an invitation to an honors convocation where the boys were recognized for their God-given gifts and challenged to do something worthwhile with them.

It was a tough, highly competitive environment, but we were thrilled with the man Nat was becoming. He appreciated intellect, had the courage to do the right thing, and included God in his daily life. He also developed a disdain for teachers who bullied and those students who judged others superficially. I loved spending uninterrupted time with him, sparring wits, having philosophical arguments, and simply comparing our day's events.

The teen years: much has been said of that phenomenon. I will never forget corralling Don after a week of travel to teach both boys to shave. He had a boy on either side of him and all three had their chins up while Don shared the finer points of a clean chin. Driver's education took a depth of courage I didn't think I possessed. Since Don couldn't resist barking orders at the newest driver, and making them unbearably nervous, the bulk of instruction fell to me. When it was time to allow them to drive to school, I sent the boys off together in one car because their schools were in the same suburb. I got so tired of their fighting over the experience that I told them I was going to drive them in myself. If it resorted to that, they'd be very, very sorry because I would bitch at them the entire drive in, and bitch at them the entire drive home. With the possibility of two hours 'bitch time' a day, they managed to resolve their differences.

The boys received the bulk of my attention, since they were at a point in their development when a lot of issues needed to be processed. Little Nessie identified with my role and was often accused of mothering them. Where they were a team of two, she was my partner. I was never quite sure whether I was the mother or she was, she was that good at looking out for me. I was achieving balance in our family life at last.

When Gib was a senior, I began searching for a postsecondary program. His development had consistently lagged behind his chronological age by two years, so it was imperative to me that he have time to finish "catching up" for his lost time. If he ended up with the skills for college, great. If not, we'd seek a working situation for him. First, we needed time to know where he stood.

Once again, I prayed fervently for guidance. We visited our top choices during spring break and returned home confident that a preparatory school in Carbondale, Illinois, was our next home. Dr. C. evaluated Gib and it was the most honest, insightful discussion we'd ever had with any professional in all of our school experiences. In fact, Dr. C. suggested Gib would have fared better in school if he'd learned sign language. I sure wish I'd thought of that one.

When the boys were in high school, they were taught meditation as a method for stress management. I was thrilled because I had practiced meditation for years and found it to be a wonderful respite. Meditation was a more mature approach to prayer for me, one that involved my listening, instead of doing all the talking, as I did in prayer. In learning to pay attention to the details of my life, I was provided guidance and answers that led me through the maze.

Gib really took prayer and meditation to heart. Every day in the late afternoon before dinner, he'd sit on his bed cross-legged, holding a rosary that Nat had brought him from a high school trip to the Vatican. He'd go into the zone, as I thought of it, a deep level of sleep where he couldn't hear or respond to us. One day I overheard his siblings complaining about him.

"Man, have you even seen Gib meditate?" Nat asked.

"Yeah, isn't it weird?" Nessie responded. "If you try to call to him for dinner, he doesn't hear you."

"Even if you shake him, he doesn't wake up," Nat laughed.

"It's so weird. I just walk away because he doesn't respond," Nessie said.

I thought back to his first 10 years of life, when waking him for a trip to the bathroom was impossible. I used to wonder where he was. The out-of-body theory was a good one for him. Funny, I hadn't thought of that in years.

One day the kids complained to me about Gib's prayer practices. "Mom," Nessie began, "you really must do something about him. I found him lying face down on the floor with his arms out like a cross. He was praying that way," she said indignantly.

"So? What harm was he doing? Was he hurting anyone?" I responded.

"Well, no, but it's weird," both kids chimed in.

"Seriously, what harm was he doing?"

"He acts like he's a monk or something," they complained.

"Leave him alone. He's entitled to pray like he wants to, and you two need to work on your tolerance," I concluded. I must admit I was amazed. I confided this latest situation to Don, my resident Catholic, as I teasingly called him.

"Hey, the kids were complaining about Gib praying face down on his carpeting," I said as we were climbing into bed.

"Really?" Don said.

"Yes, I was just wondering where he'd get the idea to do that. Who prays like that?" I figured since Don was the recipient of all that parochial and Jesuit education, he must know.

"In a prone position? Well, I guess the clergy would. I've seen pictures of priests taking their vows while they lie prone before the altar," he said.

"So, where would Gib learn about that?"

"Hm. I don't know," Don said.

"It reminds me of when he couldn't stay away from that crucifix in the art museum, and how he wouldn't part from the altar of that church in Lugano. Remember how you had to tear him away from both places? That psychic Elaine said he'd been a monk in a previous life. Maybe she was on to something."

"Maybe." Don wanted to get some sleep.

"I'm serious," I insisted. "How would he even know priests lie prone? Why would they do that?"

"To submit their will to God's," Don responded.

The impact of his words hit home for me. "He's done this before, in another time, hasn't he? This must be a past-life memory. And remember Nat, when he returned from Italy, and how enthralled he was with Assisi? He has always loved all things Italian. Maybe they really were monks together."

"Reincarnation isn't anything new, you know," he said. "The Jesuits talked about it."

"Well, I was raised Protestant, and let me tell you, that concept was never even introduced," I laughed.

"It doesn't much matter, does it?" Don said as he rolled over to turn out the light.

"It's what we accomplish in the time that we're here that counts."

CHAPTER ELEVEN

Do not fear. Only believe. All things are possible to him
that believes.

Jesus

Many times Gib would voice concern over the state of affairs in
the world. The summer after high school graduation, he became
particularly alarmed.

"There are terrorists who want to take us out, Mom. Do you
know that?" he'd fret. "People hate us."

"What people, Gib?" I asked cautiously because I was half afraid
we might have something mental going on, like paranoia or worse.

"Arabs."

"What?" One thing I can't tolerate is a bigot. I was careful to
give him the benefit of the doubt, knowing articulation wasn't his
strong point. "Arabs don't hate us. We have a huge Arab community
in Detroit. They like being here."

"Not people here. They're in the Middle East. They don't hate
you and me, they hate the U.S.," he asserted. This discussion was in
1998, before the current conflict.

"Yes, of course there are people in the Middle East who don't
like the U.S. They don't get the chance to know us personally. They
usually meet people who are greedy and who go over there to exploit
them. We can't worry about that," I reassured him. "There isn't
anything we can do from our insignificant lives."

"You don't understand," he persisted. "There are terrorists plotting to hurt us." He sounded in genuine pain.

"Gib, stop watching the news. Just because there is conflict in the world does not mean terrorists are plotting against us," I argued. These were the Clinton years, and prosperity was thundering along. I had read news articles that questioned our government's relaxed attitude about defense, and I wondered if he'd seen some of the same items.

Other times Gib would stagger down the stairs after an afternoon nap and announce, "I'm worried about tough times coming, Mom. People need to get right with God."

I sighed. "What people, us?"

"No Mom, nonbelievers. They need to know to prepare."

"For what?"

"End times. All the signs are there for the end of days."

Damn. He was reading that extreme right-wing stuff; I knew it. All the fictional end-time prophecy books capitalized on the Bible's prophecies and made people fearful.

"Gib, no one knows the day or time. No one. Stop obsessing about this end-time stuff. It's just fear mongering. And guess who feeds off fear?"

"Satan."

"Correct. Now stop it." I would try to reason him out of these episodes, but I was worried that we might have serious problems. It seemed anxiety-driven, and I was trying to catch a pattern of behavior. It was a sporadic thing. We'd be caught up in the business of living when he'd suddenly worry about the souls of others.

"Gib, what makes you think it's your job to try to save them?" I'd ask.

"Well, someone needs to tell them. People need to know," he'd insist.

"There are plenty of evangelicals in the world already. Let's mind our own business, okay?"

He'd just shake his head and move on with life, but he'd let me know he was praying for people to find their way to God. I figured that was fair enough. To my mind there was never enough prayer in the world.

The terrorist thing really irritated us. Sometimes I'd hear Nat or Nessie scold him. "Will you just shut up about the terrorists? You're driving us nuts." I considered we were dealing with mental illness, but was hesitant to medicate him just yet.

The first year we moved Gib to his new school in Illinois was tough. Don and I felt it was necessary to cut the umbilical cord to see what he could do alone. Every person reaches a point in life when he learns of the mettle he's made of, and Gib needed to dig deep and realize his potential. The school would be the safely net. It would also provide a concentrated learning environment to give some finish to his developmental gap. It would be hard, but we'd have a complete assessment of his abilities for life.

Gib was so sad when we left. We'd moved him into his bedroom in a townhouse that was home to three other boys. The counselors were next door, and every moment of his day was supervised. He was in safe, capable hands. We hugged him and went out to the car. Then Don surprised us by going back into the house for another hug. I stayed in the car so Gib couldn't see me crying.

We drove away and I cried for 100 miles. We eventually stopped for dinner, and as we sat in the restaurant, I acknowledged that I was an emotional wreck. I watched a young daddy herd his two toddler sons to their table, and my eyes brimmed with tears again.

"Look, Don, that could be you, Gibby, and Natty, as you were 15 years ago," I sniffled.

"Great," Nat announced. "Are we going to have to watch you cry forever?"

"Oh, no," I deadpanned. "Not at all. I figure I've got nothing better to do now than to give you my undivided attention." I emphasized the last two words as I gave him my steeliest look.

His face registered horror at the thought of all that unwanted attention. He gulped hard while Don just howled with laughter.

Every week Gib would phone us, telling us about his new life. The sound of grief in his voice was palpable.

"Gibby, pray for God to help you with this," I urged.

"Okay, Mom," he'd answer dully.

I'd consult with his life coaches and teachers weekly.

"He's very homesick, Sue. He misses you so much, but we're keeping him busy and reaching out for what he needs. This is normal. Don't visit for eight weeks or so. We've found that it takes that long to work through the homesickness. If you interrupt the process, you delay the adjustment." Great, but who was helping me? I felt like I had a 10-ton elephant standing on my chest.

Every Sunday we'd call him. "Mom, I miss you," he'd say. He was the saddest- sounding person I'd ever known.

"Me too, Honey," I'd chirp, trying to be upbeat and cheerful. "I'm so proud of you. This is adult stuff, you know. You're really learning to be your own man."

Silence. I could almost hear the tears falling silently down his cheeks.

"Hey! Tell me about your social activities this week. Where did you go? Did you go grocery shopping? Did you go to the mall?"

Gradually he would start talking about his life. I knew he went to a Newman Center on a neighboring college campus. One of his housemates was Catholic, so the Center provided volunteers to transport the boys. Father Greg befriended Gib, and church became a lifeline for him.

When parents weekend finally arrived, I was agitated during the entire flight. I could not wait to see our boy. We sequestered him in our motel room for the weekend so we could laugh, talk, joke, and hug, and, in my case, just watch him sleep. We attended conferences and were encouraged with his progress. When it was time to say farewell, it was tough, but we were upbeat, with assurances that he'd be home for the next holiday. Gib was diligent about marking the days off his calendar until his next visit.

I must share a bit of the magnitude of life I was living in that first year Gib was away. Not only did I feel like an elephant was sitting on my chest as I tried to cope with my first child leaving the nest, but Nathaniel was finishing a very active senior year of high school and applying to universities while Nessie was approaching her eighth-grade graduation and high school search. Don was on assignment in London, England, so he was returning home bimonthly for visits and begging me to fly to the U.K. for a long weekend with free air miles. I just could not find the time to leave the kids. I felt like a wagon master who would lose control of the team if I dropped the reins for even a second.

Don would fly out on Sunday evenings. One Monday morning I was in the kitchen preparing breakfasts and lunches with the news on the television in the background. Suddenly I noticed a huge news flash about a terrible train crash at Paddington Station in London that had just occurred. I felt the blood drain from my head. I knew Don's habit was to take the commuter train from Heathrow to Paddington Station and go directly to his office, and I was thinking the timing of the crash was pretty close to when he would be using that station.

I quickly turned off the television set and pushed that thought to the back of my mind. I didn't want to concern the kids. I saw Nat out the door as he left for school, fed Nessie her breakfast and took her to school, and then returned as quickly as I could to continue watching the news coverage.

Getting the nerve up to call London was really tough. I was afraid I wouldn't like what I heard. Finally, I called Don's London office. A colleague answered.

"Is Don there?" I rasped.

"No he isn't. May I take a message?"

"This is his wife. Did he arrive at the office this morning?" I asked, hesitantly.

"Why, yes he did. He just stepped out for a bit of lunch." I marveled at how calm this guy sounded while I felt like an imploding brick wall. "Is there anything wrong?"

"Yes. The news is showing a horrible train crash at the Paddington Station, and I wanted to be sure Don wasn't involved in it," I exhaled with relief.

"Oh my goodness, we've heard nothing about it. I will have Don call you directly," he said.

When Don called me, I cried. I just sat down by the phone and sobbed. I was never so happy to hear his voice. What would I ever do without him? Of course, Don was incredulous.

"I can't believe this," he said. "I missed that predicament by 20 minutes. I just came through there." He was amazed, freaked, grateful; so many emotions in that one short conversation. Here was another near miss for his tally sheet. He has been amazingly lucky in his lifetime.

"Just finish this assignment and get home," I said, wiping tears. "I can't be worrying about you, too." I wondered to myself how much weight I would gain from this stress-capade.

In spring 2000 we watched Nat and Vanessa graduate from their respective schools, moved Gib home for the summer, went to orientation for Nat, moved Nat to college, moved Gib to school, started Nessie at her new high school, and then I thought I might take a breath when the phone rang one morning with a dear friend calling.

"So what are you doing now that you're nearly an empty nester?" she asked.

"Wow. I haven't even thought about it. Maybe I'll get reacquainted with myself. I'm taking a watercolor class at the community center that I'm really enjoying. I still have to carpool until Nessie starts driving."

"Well, let me share with you a situation I have that might be a nice opportunity for you," she said and launched into her explanation of her job at the local land conservancy, her husband's job transferring them out of state, the wonderful board of directors she worked for, and how perfect I'd be for the job with my management and fundraising background. One haunting aspect of this conversation was the reoccurring thoughts I'd had over recent months about needing to get involved with the local land conservancy, and that I would feel remorse for not getting involved with trying to preserve some open space for future generations. Due to that pre-existing thought, I decided to follow the path to see where it led. I ended up replacing my friend as the executive director.

The second year was an easier transition for Gib when he returned to school. He was responsible and well-behaved, so he was elevated to a minimally supervised living arrangement. This meant he took care of his own living needs while his counselors kept a check on him. He was handling his own meal preparations, cleaning his apartment, doing his laundry and scheduling his time. He was working at the local Kentucky Fried Chicken and enjoyed his work there. His boss was supportive. Gib was proud of his progress, as were we.

He began attending a local Baptist church with one of his counselors. I thought this was healthy, since I was raised Protestant, but I cautioned him that if there was any "Catholic bashing," he was done.

"I'm not going to leave Father Greg," he protested. "He is my friend. I'll go to the Baptist church Sunday morning and the Newman Center that night."

"That's fine, Honey. I just want to warn you that some religions build themselves up at the expense of others, kind of a superiority complex thing, and it's wrong. All Christians are Christ's brothers, and just because one religion looks different from the others doesn't make it better. All people are God's children, so we need to respect each other and be a deserving family."

I cautioned him against bigotry. "You know how mad those televangelists make you when they talk badly about Catholics? It doesn't need to be that way. In my whole childhood, as a Lutheran, I never heard anyone bash another person's belief."

"Okay, Mom, I'll be careful," he laughed. The scary thing about finishing parenthood is making sure you've covered everything well. I knew it would kill me to have raised a bigot. One of the greatest tenets of being American is the strength of having all types of humans making up our society. That doesn't happen without a lot of respect and consideration for each other.

I remembered one of Gib's favorite teachers in high school whom another student criticized for being Jewish. Gib had quickly flown to her defense, telling the anti-Semite how ignorant he was. She was touched by Gib's defense, but the face of hatred he saw that day disturbed Gib.

Soon Gib transformed into a student of religion. His allowance was spent on books about every religion. He shared his books with his mentors, and they shared with him. He wanted to discuss religion at school, which was not an appropriate venue, and he was frustrated at the teachers' admonishments. Gib was able to pursue his discussions with the priest, the pastor, his counselor, and the school bus driver, who happened to be the pastor of his church.

When we visited we attended the Newman Center with him and loved the environment. When I entered the building, I could feel an atmosphere of love and acceptance. In fact, I felt the entire town honored God because the people there were friendly, caring, and accepting toward each other. I was convinced Gib was right where he needed to be.

One night, while we were attending a school dinner, the school bus driver made a point of seeking me out.

"I just want you to know, Mrs. Topping, that your son is walking with the Lord." He established eye contact with me, and I could see he was dead serious.

"Well, he's certainly special," I said.

"No, I'm serious. We talk quite often, and I want you to know that he is truly walking with the Lord."

I looked at him squarely, saying, "Thank you for sharing that," even though I had no idea what we were talking about. I thought to myself, what is it about this place? Most people here seem to spout about God as easily as the rest of us talk about the weather.

During our weekly phone chats, Gib shared that he was participating in Bible study at the Baptist church. Every week he had some insight to share, and it was fun having those discussions. One week that we talked, he was troubled by an anti-Catholic remark someone had made.

"What did you do about it?" I asked casually.

"I asked him how he could say that. I asked him if he'd ever been to a Catholic church, and he said no. So I invited him to attend Mass with me."

"Ha! Then what did he say?" I laughed.

"He said he couldn't do that, so I said, 'Then who are you to judge something you know nothing about? Do you think talking like that pleases Jesus? We're all his brothers, you know.' "

"Good for you, Gib." I was amazed at his response because he had a difficult time expressing himself, particularly if any emotion was involved.

The worry about terrorism still existed, and I was puzzled by it. There wasn't any talk of problems on the news at that time. What was driving those fears? I suspected he was hearing too much about the end-time prophecies, which I thought was fear mongering in a passive way. School forbade him to talk about this subject. I thought his imagination was overly stoked.

Summer 2001 was tiresome with his worrying. It wasn't compulsive or anything, he just insisted there were Middle Easterners who hated the U.S. and intended to declare a war. I'd respectfully listen for a few minutes before changing the subject.

Curiously, I had noticed a couple of small news articles that talked about security concerns. One item involved a semitrailer loaded with explosives that had been intercepted by police as it crossed into Washington State from Canada. Another mentioned the ease with which some people were getting birth certificates from Canadian clergymen so that they could obtain passports. There was concern that the Canadian border was so open. I hoped we hadn't become such free-wheelers during the booming Clinton years that we'd compromised our own safety.

Aug. 11 was an amazing morning for us. Nessie and I were in the kitchen getting ready for a busy day. I was packing last minute items for Gib's return to school the following day. Gib stumbled down the stairs in his underwear, half asleep and looking dreadful.

"Gib!" I admonished. "You can't walk around in your underwear; your sister is right here."

"Geez, Gib," she complained. "Can't you put on a robe?"

He stumbled to a chair at the table and sank into it.

"Oh my God, Mom. I was dreaming about a disaster right now. It was so awful, so real." He shook his head. "The buildings were attacked with bombs."

"You must have had a nightmare, honey," I consoled.

"No, it wasn't a nightmare. It was real. Mom, the buildings blew up and there was fire! There were explosions and screaming people. It was like a war." He put his head into his hands and started to cry.

I realized this was a significant event, like a premonition. A mere dream would not have been so vivid, or lasting, or emotional. I sat beside him at the table and put my arm around his shoulders.

"I saw the people jumping out of the building to escape. They just fell to the sidewalks. I can still hear the screams," he moaned.

"It's okay, Sweetie. You're safe now," I consoled. "When does this happen?"

"I don't know. Soon."

"Where?"

"A big city. Like New York." He shook his head while holding it in his hands. "Those poor, poor people. I just don't understand how anyone could do this to innocent people. They didn't do anything. How can they hate us so much?"

"Who?"

"The Middle Eastern terrorists." We sat at the table for an hour at least. Finally, I coaxed him into cleaning up for the day's appointments. He trudged sadly back up the stairs.

He was quiet most of the day, but when we went to my parents' house for a farewell dinner, he blurted out his dream as soon as he saw my mother. My mom was one of the safe people for Gib to talk to about his spiritual beliefs and experiences. She never judged him or silenced him; she just let him be Gib.

"Grandma, I saw the World Trade Center bombed by terrorists in my dream last night."

"What?" she looked puzzled, and I was amazed to hear him name the site for the first time. I scrambled to fill her in on our morning.

"What do you think?" Mom asked, after listening to our story.

"I don't know. This has never happened before. He doesn't have a history of predictions like this, but I feel like this is different. Who would we tell? How could he be credible?" I said.

"Yes, you're right. People would think he's flipped out."

"Gib. When we take you back to school, you must not talk of this. No one will believe you, and people will think you have a mental instability," I warned him. Gib nodded his head in agreement.

"I know. I sound nuts," he said. "I won't talk about it."

The next day we drove him to school, and there were 12 hours of driving fraught with his anxiety about terrorists.

"Mom, they're everywhere. No one is safe. Oh, how can they do this?" It was dreadful to witness his distress.

When we arrived at his school and greeted the staff, the first thing out of his mouth was his horrific dream.

"Wow, buddy. You've been watching too many doomsday movies." They laughed. I could tell he was hurt.

As soon as I could pull him aside, I said, "Look, Gib, don't be mad at them. They don't understand. How could they possibly? It's so random. We're going to pray our brains out that this doesn't happen, OK? And whenever you feel anxious or overwhelmed about it, call home. I don't care if you call every night if that's what you need to do." He nodded his head slowly and painfully.

I was so worried for him. What was going on here? He'd only dreamt this the day before, so it hadn't dimmed in his memory yet. I didn't want to rush to judgment and have him medicated if he didn't need it, but I was definitely going to monitor this.

He only called a couple of times a week, and he didn't seem to fuss too much about the terrorism. When he did need to discuss the dream, he was processing his pain and angst. He said he spent a lot of time on his knees, in the privacy of his bedroom, praying for God to help these people.

Then on a beautiful, clear September morning while driving to the office, I heard frightened voices over the radio describing a plane that had crashed into one of the World Trade Center's towers in New York City. With dismay, the announcer reported the unbelievable. A second plane had just crashed into the remaining tower. I felt stunned with disbelief. We were clearly under attack. My office neighbored the office for the local cable company, so I rushed in to watch the news on a television set.

We watched in horror. The fires burned and black smoke billowed into a cloudless, pristine sky. We watched desperate people jump to their deaths rather than die by fire. Unbelieving, we watched a tower collapse into a pile of rubble. Refugees tried to flee the area, and curiously, the city appeared to be quiet. I felt like we were hopelessly undefended, that every part of our county was easy prey. Then the second tower fell. News reports came in that a passenger jet had attacked the Pentagon as well. Another report talked about an airliner that had crashed in a field in Pennsylvania. Dear God, the monsters used us against ourselves. This was what Gib had seen in his dream. I could not imagine how he'd borne that burden.

I called Don and urged him to close his company's office and let the employees go home to their families.

"What? Detroit is just a pimple on the ass of the earth," he insisted. "Who is interested in us?"

"Well, it might interest you to know that Detroit was an industrial target in World War II, and we could also be seen as a capitalist target as well," I said. "Plus, your building is near the biggest tower complex in the city, headquarters for General Motors. Also, Detroit has the largest Arab population in the U.S. You can't tell me some of those terrorists didn't come across our relaxed borders and pass through here on their way to God knows where. How do you know those sickos aren't going to target skyscrapers in Detroit, Chicago, L.A,, or anywhere else?" I was in tears.

"Yeah, I see your point. I'll close the office," he agreed. It took hours for Don to get out of the downtown area. Traffic was gridlocked as skyscrapers emptied their inhabitants.

I called Gib's school. "Hey, I just wanted to see how Gib is handling this crisis."

"You know?" his teacher said with disbelief. "We can't believe it. This is the sort of thing that excites his imagination, so we were expecting him to be bonkers about this. But he's not. He's strangely calm."

"You know why, don't you? He had this premonition a month ago to the day. Remember when we arrived on campus and he tried to tell you about this?"

"Yes. Yes, I remember," he said. "We thought he'd been watching disaster movies."

"Can you imagine holding the burden of this knowledge for all this time?" my eyes were moist with tears.

"Wow, that's incredible." His teacher sounded amazed.

"Will you please tell him I'll call him tonight?" I concluded.

That evening I called him, and he was relieved to hear my voice.

"Mom. Now you know. I wasn't making it up."

"Honey, I never said you were."

"Yeah, but everyone else thought so. I'm tired of people thinking I'm crazy."

"Then we're both crazy, Gib. I never scoffed at your premonition."

"But you didn't believe me about the terrorists," he accused.

"How could I, Gib? We can't get into your head. We can't see what you see. There were no other indications of terrorists."

"Well, they're not done with us. They're at war with us."

"Who?"

"Iraq," he said.

"Honey, they're saying Bin Laden is taking responsibility for this."

"Well, Iraq backs him," Gib said calmly.

"What?" I insisted. "That was the Gulf War. This is something else. It's not a war; it's terrorists."

"No, Mom, it's all the same."

Before long our government claimed Saddam Hussein was behind the terrorists and also possessed weapons of mass destruction. I'd read reports of Iraqi refugees who'd made these claims for years. When our government asked to search for the weapons, the United Nations insisted it be handled through their searchers.

Gib fussed. "They're taking so long. The weapons won't even be there. They're moving them to Iran."

"Gib," I scolded. "Will you stop this paranoia? Iran isn't involved in this."

"Oh, yes they are, and Saudi Arabia is, too. They need to hurry because there are a lot of crazy people there who want to kill us.

I know; I see them in my dreams, and let me tell you, they are nuts."

"Gib, who are you telling this stuff to?"

"No one, Mom."

"Good," I cautioned. "Just tell me, okay?" I was afraid the school's staff would insist on medications. This sounded so extreme to me.

"Mom?"

"Yes, Honey."

"One thing really bothers me. Why would God show me the 9/11 destruction if I couldn't do anything about it?" I could hear the sorrow and regret in his voice.

"I don't know, sweetie. Ask Him."

Gib truly agonized over his premonition. He kept asking why God would show him the horror and not tell him what to do about it. While I was talking with close friends about this anguish, one friend volunteered to take Gib to visit a priest who understood spiritual gifts. I readily agreed because I wanted Gib to reconcile this situation and find peace of mind. When Gib returned home for the Christmas holiday, he visited the priest. If ever there was a time for spiritual advice, this was it.

Gib shared with me that the priest comforted him about the vision and explained that he was meant to pray for those souls. The power of praying assisted them in their transition to death. Given the vast numbers of deaths on that day, there was bound to be a need to help in that way. God didn't necessarily think you, Gib, could stop that event. Heaven needed your prayers.

Gib assured the priest that he prayed every day, fervently. Gib showed him the rosary Nat had brought home from a visit to the Vatican. He explained how important the rosary was to him because he held it during prayer.

I will always be thankful the priest took time for Gib. He opened up the reality to us for the power of prayer for others. We always knew to pray for those who needed help, but in this instance we saw a connection between the power of our emotion in prayer and how it helped other souls. I had never thought much about souls before.

Now my son and I were praying daily for other people's spirits with feeling and conviction.

I also spent time thinking about Gib's psychic gifts. He'd demonstrated abilities as a small child, but during the strife of his school years, those tendencies had seemed to disappear. Now they were back. It was not the sort of talent that is common, although I suspected that it would be more so if people weren't so afraid of everything.

Undoubtedly, there is a shadow side of spirituality in the negative forces, but I hardly feel we are best served by living in so much fear we ignore our sixth sense, our spiritual connection. If the spirit exists, then God had to have created it. I began to view religion as a device to protect ourselves, but I also believe that, in the fervor to protect, we fail to acknowledge the purpose of spirit. Spirit is the breath of God, and in our fear we take shallow breaths, failing to take the deep breath that would sustain us.

As I considered Don and my children, I realized I'd instinctively taught them to protect themselves with God's pure light, and to believe totally and without doubt that upon asking, they would enjoy His protection. No wonder they were loving and centered.

Every day I spent time in deep thought, as if I were finally assimilating all the knowledge I'd been putting in my head for all these years.

CHAPTER TWELVE

Life is not measured by the number of breaths we take but
by the moments that take our breath away.
George Carlin

One cold Saturday morning in March, I found myself at a planning seminar that related to my work at the land conservancy. I was sitting at a round table with my dear friend Sue on my right and a pleasant-looking woman, older than me by about 15 years, on my left. As the first speaker began at 8 a.m. sharp, I felt horrified that I had given up my day off to sit in this room. I closed my eyes and silently said to God, "Okay, Lord. What on earth am I doing in this seminar after my 50-hour workweek? This doesn't make sense to me, and I'm too tired to be here."

No sooner had I completed my prayer than I became aware of the lady seated next to me. I looked and instantly realized she was our school psychologist from the POHI years, the very one who had doubted Gib's intelligence. The very one who had told staff at the children's hospital about our trip to Europe. The same one had who voiced an opinion that Barb was unstable, which led to assertions that Barb was an unfit mother for Danny.

Whoa. For many years I had prayed to be a servant to God, and I knew what this was. I closed my eyes and prayed again. "All right, Father. I will be your mouthpiece, but only if you choose the words and you protect me."

I then leaned forward to Sue and whispered, "I am so freaked out right now. Remind me to tell you about the woman seated next to me." Sue gave me a quizzical look.

At the midmorning break, I turned to the woman and said, "Aren't you Mrs. Smart?

"Why, yes I am, and you are?" she smiled.

"Sue Topping. You might remember my son, Gibby Topping. You conducted his psychological testing for the POHI program in the mid 1980s. We disagreed about your methodology," I said.

"Yes, I do remember you. How is he doing?"

"Fine. He has learning disabilities, but other than that he's functioning well. Fortunately, we were able to send him to private schools that specialized in intelligence development, so his self-esteem is intact."

"What about that other little boy that your son was friendly with?" She clearly didn't have Gib's welfare in mind.

"Danny?"

"Yes, that's the one. I heard he died," she stated simply.

"Yes, he did, and not through any fault of his parents. We should all be so lucky to have such dedication."

"They took their son to Switzerland for treatment, didn't they?"

I thought to myself, *I get it Lord. I know what this is about.* I took a deep breath and launched into an abridged version of the story without assuming she knew the details. *Let her judge her own actions*, I thought.

"Yes, and so did we. The treatment absolutely saved Gib's life. We've no doubt he would be in a wheelchair by now if we hadn't gone. In fact, my husband received the treatment as well. His immune system was compromised, and the treatment helped him tremendously. Our doctor was a member of the World Health Organization and affiliated with the Louis Pasteur Laboratories, so this was hardly quackery. In fact, our American doctors should have had such credentials," I laughed. "Do you know that while Barb and I sat in his office with our sons, a leading university medical school consulted our doctor on the phone about the uses of human placenta

in helping cystic fibrosis? Shortly after our return from Europe we heard the news announcement that a treatment had been found."

"No. Really?" she seemed very interested.

"Yes. Pretty cool, eh? The treatment worked perfectly for Gib. Unfortunately for Danny, the treatment didn't help him. He had a birth defect, and the damage was permanent."

"Oh, dear," she sympathized.

"You want to hear something heinous? Barb had exhausted all the doctors she had been referred to, and Dan just kept getting sicker. A prominent toxicologist suggested she take him to a particular hospital, and she begged for someone to help her little boy. His liver had high mercury content, and when they chelated the mercury, it went into the bloodstream and did massive damage to his brain stem.

"Someone called the hospital and told the doctors Barb was so unstable a mother that she fed him a protein diet, and she took him out of the country for medical treatment. They all decided she had Munchausen's syndrome by proxy and took custody of Danny away from her because he had been adopted, which in their feeble minds proved she couldn't possibly love him like her own. Isn't that evil? Can you imagine someone else defining her ability to love? It was in all the newspapers at the time. Surely you read of it."

She shook her head in amazement.

"My husband and I were subpoenaed to testify on her behalf. We had received the treatment, too. I followed a strict rotation diet with whole foods for Gib's allergies. Was I going to lose custody for being perceived a nut, too? Fortunately, the judge dismissed most of the case."

I could not believe the ease with which my words passed out of my mouth. They were coming faster than I could think of them.

"Want to hear the real kicker?" I said incredulously. "Somebody looked up the adoption papers and contacted the birth mother, saying that her son was the abuse case in all the papers. On top of Barb's son being blind and in a vegetative state, being fed by a feeding tube in a foster home where he knew no one, Barb had to deal with the histrionic accusations of this woman who had damaged her baby in the first place. This unwed mother had smoked pot and drank alcohol while the baby was in uterus, and she'd thrown him off the porch in a temper fit.

"Years later Barb read a report that marijuana grown in Hawaii in volcanic soil had high mercury content, which was poisoning users. Also, the drug companies were using mercury as a preservative in vaccines and the disposable diaper industry was using mercury, as well. Here was Barb, just trying to help the poor child, and she was persecuted."

"Wow," she said, looking amazed by my recapitulation. I was dazed at how succinctly the basics of that story were presented. Everything seemed to flow effortlessly through my mouth. I felt disengaged, as though the story was not about me at all. I simply got out of the way. I didn't make any judgments. I didn't make any assumptions. It was what it was.

"Well," I continued speaking, "hopefully some good came from it all. I've heard that experts now acknowledge that mercury should no longer be used in the manufacture of disposable diapers. They can't prove it, but they suspect there may be a mercury-related link between vaccinations and autism. Poor Danny, with his unique situation, didn't stand a chance. I'd like to think that someone at the hospital reviewed Danny's case, put two and two together, found the mercury link with other stray cases, and initiated a change in policy for the manufacturers."

We heard the conference moderator beseeching all of us to take our seats. "Goodness," Mrs. Smart said as we moved to sit down. "That's quite a story."

"Let me tell you, it was absolute hell to live through," I agreed. "It was dreadful how quickly everyone rushed to judgment of Barb."

As the speaker resumed his topic, I marveled at what had just transpired. I silently prayed, *Thank you, Lord, for being with me and guiding my words. Let this have been for the higher good of all involved.* Out of the corner of my eye, I could see Mrs. Smart peeking looks at me. The look on her face kept changing. I thought each look revealed another insight as her memory replayed itself. By lunchtime, she dismissed herself and left the conference. I sincerely hoped this situation had occurred for her best interest.

When I arrived home, I thundered into the den where Don was working.

"You'll never guess who I sat next to today," I said and launched into the events of the morning.

"Did you claw her eyes out?" he kidded.

"No. That's the surprising part. I was completely devoid of emotion. I simply stated the facts for her personal use. I told God I would be his vehicle if he chose my words carefully and protected me. It was brilliant. I didn't accuse or judge; I just laid out the facts of the total story."

"What do you think she thought?" he asked.

"I don't have a clue. It's none of our business, really. Maybe she needs to learn something from this; I don't know. It's obviously between her and the Lord. Man, I've got to call Barb. She won't believe this." I scurried from the room to dial Barb.

"Hi, you," she said.

"Barb, you'll never guess what!" I said, launching into the whole story. I don't think I took a breath the entire time, I was so amazed.

"Thank you, thank you, thank you," she calmly said. I had always felt saddened by the amount of fatigue in Barb's voice over the years. "I couldn't have done it. I don't have the strength anymore. At last I feel like the truth was heard."

"Don't thank me, thank God. I'm serious. I cannot take credit for any of it. I was stunned to run into her at an urban planning seminar, after all these years. What are the chances of that? And what are the chances of being able to encapsulate those events and communicate quickly and succinctly, during a 15-minute break, no less.

"It's amazing; it really is," she agreed.

"When I pray to God, I frequently ask Him to let me be his servant. I really believe this was His work. I'm thinking the woman needed to hear the entire story for some reason." After I hung up with Barb, I carefully reviewed the circumstances. I pondered the enormous coincidence of it all, and then considered what a coincidence really was. Maybe the word means different things to different people, but in view of my past, I had to admit that my coincidences ended up being for my own good. Has it always been the hand of God? What an enormous oversight, then, to explain away in manmade terms something that was divine. I was beginning to sincerely feel like a sinner. It was egocentric to discount God's workings in my life.

A few months after the planning seminar experience, I was seated next to a charming lady at my friend's bridal shower for her daughter. We hit it off well and found that we both had learning-disabled sons. My new acquaintance shared a horror story that concerned a particularly arrogant school psychologist who had dismissed the mother's input because she wasn't a professional.

I was more than intrigued. "Do you remember her name?" I asked.

"Certainly." She divulged the name of our same misguided "professional," Mrs. Smart. I was dismayed how one person could adversely affect so many lives. I concluded that this latest coincidence was my personal affirmation that my past encounter at the seminar was divinely inspired. I quietly expressed my gratitude to God for allowing me to be His servant.

CHAPTER THIRTEEN

Discovery consists of seeing what everybody has seen and
thinking what nobody else has thought.

Jonathan Swift

When Gib left Brehm Preparatory School that spring, it was his
final goodbye. Every person who had been involved with him was
exemplary: the staff, his employers, his priest, and his pastor. I
appreciated them all and was thankful to the very core of my being.
We had been put in the right place for Gib's circumstances. I was
really worried to have the ball back in my court, however.

The first order of business was to find a church where we felt a
strong spiritual connection. I hadn't been happy with our parish since
the pious people had run out the wonderful priest we'd had. They
couldn't deal with Vatican II changes he had incorporated after the
old priest died. We were deeply ashamed to be in the congregation
the day he announced his departure. We felt Gib needed to replace
the church connection he'd enjoyed while away. He deserved it, and
so did we. Our neighbor enjoyed a different parish. That church
integrated music into the Mass in a very meaningful way. We visited
one Sunday morning, and the minute we sat down, Gib said he
heard "Welcome home" in his mind. When I received communion
and returned to my seat, I prayed for a while, as is my custom. This
time I agonized over my next course of action with Gib. We were
standing at the crossroads again, and I felt uncertain about what to
do next for him.

Dearest Father, I prayed with emotion. How many times have I burdened him with my worries, heartbreak, confusion, and frustration? *What do I do now? Where do I take him? What does he need?*

Relax. It's not your problem anymore.

I was stunned. I knew I didn't own that thought. I sat there quietly considering the message. My first inclination was to assume I'd imagined everything. When I succeeded in talking my all-knowing ego out of ownership, I was forced to consider the presence of God. *Well, OK, I will follow my guidance. Thank you.* I felt truly humbled.

The sanctuary of this church continually filled my vessel. I always managed to hear the right message, the necessary reading, or the perfect lyric to direct me. I always asked God to let me carry His light for others. My spirituality was growing by leaps and bounds, but I was my own worst enemy with my fears. Those fears gnawed away at my confidence. How do you know you're not being led astray? How can you be sure it's really God? What makes you so sure it's not your ego? What makes you think God would talk to you? Good heavens, the battles we inflict on ourselves. I finally stripped away the fears with the simple logic that since I'd asked God for the guidance, I needed to employ faith in Him.

Yet living with Gib was an undeniable experience. He would tell me of seeing Jesus in his dreams and that Jesus would tell him not to be afraid, He was with him. Or that Jesus would say, "I'm here for everyone. All people have to do is ask me into their lives." When Gib shared these experiences, I'd think, "How wonderful." Before long the old doubts would whittle away at me. "What? Why would Jesus be talking to Gib?" In reality, why wouldn't He? Why wouldn't He talk to any of us?

My prayers that day in our new church were answered quickly when a friend called me to ask what my plan was for Gib now that he was home. She happened to have a friend who was a counselor specializing in employment guidance. This woman quickly found him a wonderful job working for a bakery, making bread. Gib loved his job.

My friend Sue called to insist I meet a friend of hers. Her friend Rosemary was a lovely lady who also had psychic experiences. "You two need to meet," she said. "You have so much in common. I just feel I need to connect the two of you."

Since all three of our daughters attended the same high school, fate finally found us one day waiting in our cars in the parking lot. I must say that when I met Rosemary, I saw the same white light around her eyes that I hadn't seen in years.

Gib had received a temporary layoff from his job and accompanied me one day when I picked up his sister. Sue was delighted to see him and stood at his car window visiting. Rosemary was next to my window, and I introduced her to my son. Her face lit up with surprise. She kept giving me a wide-eyed look of astonishment, so I told her I'd call her later in the day.

"Okay, do you want to tell me what that was about?" I laughed when she answered her phone.

"Uh, I'm not sure," she said. "I need to have someone else take a look at him. I have a dear friend who happens to be a well-known psychic. She works with the police and has been on the radio. Do you mind if I invite her to meet your son?"

"OK," I agreed. "Just let me know when and where."

"I'm also thinking of including some other friends of mine who are gifted. Let me see if I can pull this group together and get back with you," Rosemary said. I was really looking forward to this experience.

Rosemary organized a group meeting for a few consecutive weeks, and I was amused that the schedule coincided with Gib's layoff time. I was now at the point in my spiritual evolution that I could acknowledge a problem as an opportunity. I included Barb in the group. She had recently moved home from her husband's job assignment in Japan, and she knew everything about Gib, anyway. I would value her input.

Rosemary's friend, Cassia, was a little ball of energy. I enjoyed meeting every member of that group. They tended to be people who had experienced a few miracles of their own. It didn't take long for Cassia to position Gib against a wall so that everyone could look at his aura.

I must say I've never had luck with seeing the energy field around a person. I've known several folks whom I really respected who could see, so I was totally accepting of that concept. I'd seen pictures of auras captured with Kirlian photography, and they included many different colors. Since I didn't possess that particular talent, I sat in a chair out of the way and prepared to wait.

I heard Gib whisper, "Grandpa is here," before I overheard the comments from everyone in the room. Others were describing what they saw, and from their descriptions it did sound like Don's father. I remembered Gib telling me that Grandpa often visited him during prayers or dreams, especially during his homesickness episodes while away at school. *This is interesting. I wonder if he'll see the other one he talks about*, I thought, thinking of Jesus. Gib was particularly fond of the Christ and talked to him daily in prayer.

The room was fairly quiet, and I could hear the occasional whisper between a few people when I became aware of a white glow in the corner of the room. Gradually it moved closer, then closer still. I saw a blue outline of light along Gib's left side, until the white light moved behind Gib. To my eyes, Gib became an outline within this huge white light, and I heard him softly murmur, "Jesus is here." No one else heard him because people were so busy talking among themselves.

"Wow, are you seeing what I'm seeing?" I heard someone say.

"Uh, yeah. Are you seeing Christ?" was the answer.

"Yes."

"Hey," someone else called out. "Am I losing it? I think I'm seeing Jesus."

"You're not crazy," he was answered. "I'm seeing him, too."

Everyone stood for the longest time, just looking straight ahead at Gib, alone with his or her own thoughts. When we decided to return to our homes, we shuffled out of the building in silence. I think everyone was stunned. We didn't know what to say after something like that.

As we drove away, I asked Barb if she saw anything, and she agreed that she'd seen Him.

"Gib, how do you know when it is Jesus?" I asked.

"Because I feel complete love and peace," he answered, as if this were perfectly normal. I didn't know what to think about this. I thought long and hard about what was happening to us. Why us? Who else had these experiences? I didn't know who to talk to about it all. We sounded completely mad.

When Don and I prepared to go to bed that night, I knew I needed to confide in him. If Don didn't agree with something, or if it sounded crazy, he'd let me know it.

"Look," I said emphatically. "I'm going to tell you what happened tonight. It's important to bring you along on the chronology of all this, but the minute you laugh at it I will cut you out. This stuff is dead serious."

Don looked a little hurt. "What makes you think I would laugh?"

"Don. This stuff is so incredible sounding, no one will believe it." I launched into an explanation of the evening.

"You're right," Don concluded. "Who would believe it?"

"I'm not making this up. I'm not even interpreting it. I'm just stating the facts."

"I didn't say that you were. But you have to admit, it will sound nuts to people."

"Then that's their problem. Don, how can we keep this to ourselves? I have always shared what I've learned with others in case they're meant to hear truth in it for themselves. I can't worry about whether they think I'm nuts or not. The ones who are meant to understand it will. The others I'm not responsible for. They can find their own truths."

"Yeah, but it still sounds nuts," Don agreed.

"But you know? Gib has always maintained that Jesus tells him He is here for everyone. People just need to ask Him into their lives. Whoever thinks to do that? Have we? For all our prayers to God, do we listen to Him?" I asked. It was very hard to quiet my mind that night to get some sleep.

The evening to reconvene with Rosemary and her friends arrived, and as I entered our house that afternoon, Gib met me at the door.

"Hey, Mom. I saw Jesus again during my meditation," he announced.

"Really?" I was amazed at the difference a few weeks make. Here I was, actually believing him.

"Yeah, I invited him to join us tonight," he said.

"That's nice, Honey," I responded. This was an amazing concept to me. Whoever thinks to invite Jesus anywhere? "Say Lord, want to go to a party with me tonight? I'm having a few people over tonight; care to join us?" I was mentally giggling.

Sure enough, when we joined the others, Gib announced that he wanted everyone to see Jesus again, and there He was. None of us knew what to make of this phenomenon, but we knew it meant something big. He must be appearing to us for a reason, but He wasn't telling us why. I guess we would have to figure that out for ourselves.

—

Our family vacation that summer was spent cruising the Great Lakes on our boat. No sooner had I tied us up to our slip in the marina than my cell phone rang.

"Good, you're back," my sister announced. "You might want to stop by the hospital to see Dad on your way home. He's in adrenal failure and not expected to make it."

She sounded tired, numb, and beyond. I grabbed a few necessary items, climbed into the car, and drove to his bedside. I was stunned. He was struggling, and I couldn't believe that one week ago I was talking to him.

The doctors were giving up. There was nothing to be done. It was numbing to sign the papers for Dad's release to a nursing home and hospice care. His advanced Parkinson's disease was wreaking havoc with his congestive heart failure and diabetes.

One morning Rosemary called me. "Hey, I think your dad would benefit from Reiki. Would he be open to it?"

"Let me ask, but I'm pretty sure he would. I've kept my family members up on my spiritual experiences, and they've been pretty open-minded," I said. I knew Reiki was a version of the Healing Hands method used in some hospitals to bring relief to a person's suffering. It is prayerful, and practitioners scan the body's energy field with their hands.

The day we gave Dad Reiki in the nursing home was amazing. Gib, Mom. and I sat near the bed in prayer while Rosemary and her friend Courtney practiced Reiki. Dad's room felt warm with love. When it was over, he opened his eyes and said he felt wonderful. That was the day he decided to get well, and a few weeks later he was discharged from hospice care and the nursing home.

When Dad had follow-up visits to his doctors, they were astounded by his recovery. They declared that they rarely see this sort of turnaround.

"To what do you attribute this miracle, Cliff?" one doctor asked.

"I tell you, don't ever underestimate the power of prayer," Dad answered.

Needless to say, I started reading everything I could find about esoteric energy.

CHAPTER FOURTEEN

What you love, you empower. And what you fear, you
empower. And what you empower, you attract.
Unknown

When Don and I started a remodeling project for our home, we
employed a talented designer to help us. One dreary morning we met
at a tile distributor's store to make selections. Almost immediately
Patty blurted out that she'd just visited a psychic for the first time
and was amazed by the experience. She asked my opinion.

"Yes, I've heard of your psychic," I said. "She is reputable. I have
had a couple of experiences of my own. I think we need to be careful
about these things so that we don't fall under the wrong influence.
The Bible cautions against it, and it is wise advice, yet I don't think
He stopped talking to us or sending guidance because the Bible was
finished. There have been times when I've felt guided to someone
with psychic ability who has told me what I've needed to hear, and
it has been extremely helpful."

I forged ahead telling about a few of my experiences. "Some
people might want to live their entire lives with readings and not
take responsibility for their own journey through life. I don't think
that helps us with what we should learn. On the other hand, if you're
not in tune with God and receiving His guidance, you might need
to avail yourself of someone's gift to help convey a message to you.
It can be wonderful. Just know that some are influenced from the

shadow side." It was a challenge to talk about all I'd learned over the past 20 years.

"I ask God daily to protect me from everything that is not for the highest good of all and ask that the source be from Him only. Then I just trust what comes." I summarized my concern for safety.

Patty and I began meeting at a diner for breakfast to share our stories. Patty was also very open-minded about other religions. I was happy to have a nonjudgmental friend to talk to about my spiritual journey.

One morning the topic was about how Jesus' teachings can benefit us. "I'm telling you, the more I learn, the more His teachings make sense to me," I said. "There is new insight. Like 'turn the other cheek.' Who in his or her right mind can do that? But when you understand the chakra system, any fear, anger, or negative emotion is going to block your energy flow. If you're not open, you can't fully receive the life force, or God, if you will. So if you don't turn the other cheek, you are only impeding yourself."

I was really on a roll. "When Jesus instructed us to love one another, it was because of the incredible energy that love exudes. It is the emotion that puts us in connection with God. I'm sorry; I don't mean to preach Christ to you. It's just that I'm amazed at how my comprehension has shifted." Patty nodded her head. "Gib feels Christ is already back. For all the talk about Him coming again, it occurs to me that He comes from within us. Once you truly trust your connection to God, you can feel all that heaven has to offer."

We were really having a deep, heartfelt discussion. The diner was bustling with activity and was filled to capacity. It was noisy with conversation and laughter.

A little old man approached our table.

"Excuse me, ladies. I have to share a little story with you," he began. "I read it in 'Readers Digest,' and it's really cute. A little girl lost her first tooth. She carefully bundled it up and put it under her pillow." I smiled because I had read the story myself, and it was a cute one. The man was facing Patty and directing his words more to her than to me. She had a surprised and delighted look on her face as she listened.

"So when the mother sneaked into her room to switch the tooth for money, the little girl awakened," he continued. "She sat up in bed and confronted her mother. 'I caught you stealing from the tooth fairy. Now you put that back!' Isn't that cute?" the man roared with laughter.

"Thank you for sharing that story," we said. "Laughter is wonderful medicine."

"Yes it is. Well, you two ladies have a nice day." He walked away. Patty slipped out of the booth to make a dash for the restroom. I sat at the table watching the man gather his coat and limp out of the diner. I appreciated his caring and issued a mental prayer. *God bless you,* I prayed for him. *God bless you.*

I was surprised at the love I felt for him as I watched him move toward his car. I was amazed at the power I felt, the energy of the emotion. My heart felt expanded, as though energy was emanating from it. When he turned to open his car door, I was stunned to see a gigantic crucifix necklace hanging around his neck. Why hadn't I seen that before?

When Patty returned to our table, I leaned forward and whispered.

"What WAS that?"

"I don't know," she laughed.

"I just watched him walk to his car. Did you see his necklace? Who wears stuff like that?"

"Didn't you see it when he was at our table?" Patty asked. "It was eye level to me; I couldn't help but notice it."

"No, I didn't see it. He was turned toward you. How did he know we were having a Jesus discussion? Was he behind us? Could he hear us?"

"I don't see how," she said. "He was way back in the corner."

"And what did that story mean, exactly? It was like a parable for faith or something," I insisted.

"I don't know," she said. "I'm so amazed by this. I'm not real big on the Christ thing. Maybe I should be."

"Man. What a coincidence. But then, there is no such thing as coincidence. There's a purpose to everything, and this is just one more example of divine intervention," I laughed. "Well, I suspect it will all reveal itself in due time." We slid out of the booth and paid our bills, just looking at each other with our mouths hanging open.

A week later Don and I ate breakfast in the same restaurant. We were talking about the problems in the world and the lack of patience people have with each other. It felt like life's pressures were mounting. We both acknowledged seeing more incidences of road rage when driving. The newspapers informed us of greater atrocities in American society.

"Well," I interjected, thinking of my heightened relationship with God, "it makes me grateful that Christ is with us and at work in the world."

Imagine my shock when the same little old man came into the diner and sat himself behind Don, facing me. "Don!" I whispered in disbelief. "There's the man I told you about. Remember me telling you about the guy with the crucifix around his neck who told us the tooth fairy joke? What are the chances of seeing him again?"

"I'd say the chances are pretty slim," Don agreed. Don rose to visit the restroom so that he could get a good look. While he was gone, the old man saw me watching him and smiled.

"I like your necklace," I managed to say.

"Why, thank you. You know, this was given to me many years ago as a gift, and I always wore it under my shirt. I was afraid I might offend. Recently, I decided to wear it openly, and I'm pleased to say I've had positive results." I could tell he was quite proud of himself.

When Don returned we resumed eating our breakfast. After finishing and preparing to leave, I glanced back and said goodbye to the old gentleman.

"God bless you," he said simply. I was awed. It was the very blessing I'd issued him at our last encounter. How many people offer blessings to each other?

"Thank you," I said and mentally thanked God for my many blessings. I never saw the old man again.

CHAPTER FIFTEEN

All that we are is the result of what we have thought. The
mind is everything. What we think we become.
Buddha

When our sessions with Rosemary finished, Gib was coincidentally
called back to his job. I continued my prayers and meditations,
fervently asking for answers to this quandary. Why was our son so
spiritual? Was he gifted because he was shorted on language ability,
or was he shorted on language ability because he was gifted? Why
was this happening to me? I didn't see where I was particularly
capable of helping Gib through this. Honestly, I considered myself
a mongrel Christian. I was a composite of my ancestry: Lutheran,
Methodist, Quaker, and Catholic. I respect all religions and consider
"relationship" to be the key component. My credo has always been
to "be in relationship with God," and that's the way we've raised our
children. All men are brothers; it doesn't matter what their colors
are. I just can't understand why hair, eye, or skin coloring matters to
anyone. It's such a shallow value. I also feel all people who believe in
God are our cousins. I'd never discussed my beliefs with friends, it
just was. So what was happening with this Jesus stuff?

I corralled a trusted friend who was a doctor of psychology to
tell him about these recent developments. "I know what a Christ
complex is. I know about delusions, schizophrenia, and all the usual
mental disorders. So tell me, should I be concerned? Am I losing
it?" I asked.

"No," he said. "You are the most practical, logical, sane person I know. The fact that you're telling me these things gives me hope."

Needless to say, I was thankful for his confidence.

I asked Cassia to spend some time with Gib. She sought me out afterward for counsel.

"Let me tell you, when he says he's talking to Jesus, he is REALLY TALKING TO JESUS. OK? So you need to get over it," she said emphatically. "Also, there is a story that needs to be told. Why hasn't it?"

"Well, there certainly is a story in regard to Gib's health," I began, "but in the end it's become more of a story about the journey of my faith." I was realizing this for the first time.

"Exactly," Cassia nodded. "That's the story you must write. Promise, right now, that you will publish this in a book."

"I promise," I said.

When I was by myself, I started another conversation with God. *Okay Lord, I hear You now.* Cassia was right; I needed to get over my problems with it. Gib sees Jesus. I was amazed to realize I did indeed have a problem accepting it, but I also knew I had never discounted it to anyone else. I kept my doubts to myself. How did she know that?

—

Christmas Eve that year was a memorable evening for us. As we opened the door to our family members arriving for holiday dinner, Gib took me aside and looked at me with sheer anxiety.

"Mom, something bad is about to happen."

"What?" I said urgently.

"I don't know. After 9/11 I asked God not to show me the details if I couldn't do anything about it." I certainly couldn't blame him for asking to be freed of that burden.

"Where does it happen?" I asked. "Are we in danger?"

"No."

"Anyone we know?"

"No," he tousled his hair. "I just know it's huge and involves a lot of people. I woke from a nap hearing water rushing and people screaming." He looked so sad.

"Well, Sweetie, we know what to do, don't we. Start praying."

He nodded his head glumly, and with that my parents stepped into the foyer and our Christmas festivities began.

The next day the news told us of a terrible tsunami in the Indian Ocean that killed thousands of people. We prayed for those souls. One day Gib announced, "Mom. It's a real mess. When I pray I can hear children crying. The ones who are here cry for their dead parents, and the dead children cry for their living parents. I saw Jesus and asked him to send their ancestors to help them find their way."

"Boy, Gib, that's really thoughtful."

"You know what he said?" Gib smiled. "He said, 'You don't need to worry about the children; they are with me.' Isn't that cool?"

"Yes, that is really awesome."

I began to share some of these stories with my parents and sisters. I guess I didn't feel I should sit on the information, and I've always had confidence in myself. I couldn't worry about looking nuts anymore. This stuff was important enough to share with others.

"Do you expect me to believe Jesus is talking to Gib?" one sister scoffed.

"I don't give a shit what you believe," I retorted. "I'm just telling you in case you need to know." I guess that's been my attitude about sharing information. There may come a time when this will mean something to someone. It's not my job to filter knowledge. I don't want to be guilty of having more fear of ridicule than faith in God's grace.

—

The hurricane season that year was awful for Florida, just as Gib had warned the previous year. After the last major storm of the season, Gib said, "That's nothing. Wait until you see the one that takes out New Orleans." I just looked at him. I knew he'd just passed significant information on to me again.

—

Rosemary was a Reiki master and offered to give me a session. I was already familiar with Reiki, since Don had shared what he'd learned in Japan and Taiwan about energy work all those years ago when he'd traveled. He was amazed when he saw people standing on a street corner having their Chi adjusted. Energy work was commonplace.

My dad's experience was miraculous. Reiki taps into the universal life force and flows through the practitioner to the client. There was no doubt in my mind that the universal life force was of God. He is the Source for everything. You don't have to be a rocket scientist to understand that every living thing inputs and outputs energy. We all know what splitting an atom can do. I also knew that "healing touch" was being utilized in hospitals and in hospice care, so the idea was transitioning from the East to Western acceptance.

I loved Reiki. I found that 20 minutes of lying on a massage table with some soothing music in my ear does wonderful things to my disposition. The practitioner scans your auric field for the length of your body with the palms of his or her hands. Occasionally I'd feel warmth where their hands had been positioned. Afterward, I felt so light on my feet and relaxed. It was better than a massage in terms of relaxation.

During one of my sessions I had a peculiar meditation. I saw a woman approach me. When she stood before me, I saw she was a young, pretty, simply clothed female in biblical attire. In her extended left hand she offered me a rosary. I understood her to be presenting herself as a dear friend who knew me intimately. I thought she could be a young version of Mary, but I wasn't sure. My upbringing didn't leave me with the need to venerate His mother at all.

As I reached for the rosary, a prayer device that I'm not familiar with, I asked her mentally what she wanted.

We want you to heal His people is what I understood.

How will I know who they are? I thought.

We will put them before you.

How will I know what to do? I asked.

I will be with you, just as I always have.

When my Reiki was finished and I awoke from my dream state, I was totally amazed at what my imagination was capable of conjuring up. I shared the experience with Rosemary. "Wow, what an imagination I have! Listen to this," I said as I launched into the details of my fantastical dream.

Three days later I was rooting around in old cabinets looking for diaries I kept during Gib's early years, and I stumbled upon a manila envelope. When I peered inside, I was amazed.

Fifteen years previously, when I attended business meetings in California with Don, I met a woman who investigated miracles for the Catholic Church. She seemed so serene, and every time I looked at her I saw white light above her head. I was perplexed enough to mention this occurrence to her while at a cocktail party. She smiled and told me about her line of work. When Americans returned from Medjugorje, Bosnia-Hercegovina, and claimed to experience a miracle, she interviewed them and submitted her report to the church. We talked about my faith experience with Gib and his medical treatment. She felt that Gib had a divine purpose and wondered if she could send me some information. I agreed and gave her our address.

The manila envelope that I rediscovered was the packet sent for my perusal. I was not comfortable with its contents: prayer beads, prayer cards, photos of a Christ statue bearing scourge marks, and a taped story of the Virgin Mary vision in Medjugorje. I couldn't comprehend what I referred to as "Catholic paraphernalia," but neither could I throw it away. I don't mean to sound disrespectful about this stuff. I wasn't raised Catholic so I didn't have any value for these objects. Yet this packet had even survived a move with us, and here it was, fifteen years later, in my lap, three days after my dream. I was astounded by the coincidence.

What a wild experience this was. *The next thing I need is a Mary statue*, I laughed to myself.

The next morning, following my shower, I looked at a shelf in my bathroom and thought, *"That would be a good spot for a Mary statue to remind yourself of her."*

What? Where did that idea come from? This was confirming to me that I was losing it. I had never judged others who used statuary to remind themselves of religious characters, but it wasn't my style. That same day my friend Jill called.

"Hey there," she began. "Can you meet for lunch? I've got a little gift for you."

"Sure. I'm not busy tomorrow."

"Great." We firmed up the time and place.

When we met, I slid into my seat while she promptly produced a small gift bag. I opened it, continued to make small talk, and stopped midsentence as I unfolded a small statue of Mary. I looked at it dumbly.

"Listen. There's a story to this," Jill said hesitantly. "I hope you don't mind this little statue. I was in Sedona, Arizona, on vacation a year ago and was looking around in a gift shop. I noticed this statue of Mary, it looked all glittery and pretty, and I thought, 'I need to buy this for Sue Topping.' When I brought it home, my husband thought I was crazy. We're Protestant, so I don't usually do these things, but I told him I felt you had to have this. He insisted that we didn't know your beliefs, that this might be inappropriate, so I tucked it in a drawer and forgot about it. Lately it has bothered me that I still had this, so I thought you might like to have it."

I sat there in tears, trying to collect my thoughts. My cutoff point for affirming divine interaction for myself is three times.

"Wow, Jill. Thank you for this. You can't believe how much this means to me right now." I launched into the past week's events.

"You mean to tell me I bought this statue over a year ago so it could mean something in this moment?" Jill puzzled.

"It's divine guidance, Jill. How could that lady in California know that her package of information would be needed in 15 years?" This was incredible. We sat there and looked at each other.

The following day, Don returned from a business trip. I followed him into our bedroom to recount my fantastic Mary stories.

"Babe," I breathed. "What are the chances of three Mary stories in such a short period? I'm really blown away by this."

"Wow, Honey, it is really amazing," he agreed.

"I know! I'm not sure I know what to do next." Almost immediately I felt the urge to meditate.

"Oops, got to go pray now!" I stated, rushing off to my favorite chair. "I feel like I have incoming information." Don looked at me quizzically.

I was no more seated in my chair with my eyes closed than a picture formed in my mind. I was seeing a topographical map, and above it, in the sky, was a large bubble. Within that bubble were Jesus, Mary, Joseph, the Disciples, the Saints, and angels. Let me tell you, my knowledge about saints and angels is limited but it seemed as though anybody who was anyone important was in that bubble. About seven thin threads descended from this bubble to the earth, and the topographical map showed me that one thread connected to our home. Jesus was at the forefront of that group, and as He looked at me he said,

You're on a need-to-know basis.

I sat there for the longest time trying to understand the full scope of this message and the recent spiritual events that I had experienced. I questioned every aspect of it, like a good skeptic would. What about authenticity? How can I be sure of the source? Then I scolded myself for not accepting the truth. I'd prayed to be of service since Gib's medical crisis was past, and here was the mission. I battled my ego. How can I give over control of my life to anything or anyone? Control issues were huge for me. No wonder God can't work with ego. He can't get through to us.

One morning I looked at that little statue of Mary and thought, *This is it. Put up or shut up. The Father sent Mary to you. How on earth will you stand before Him for judgment and account for the fact that even Mary wasn't enough for you to believe?*

"Okay, Father. I submit to Your will only. Please protect me, and please guide me so that I don't lead anyone astray." I truly wouldn't want my ego to interfere and grab hold of me. This was to be God's work, not mine.

A week later Rosemary called to say it was time that I learned Reiki.

My life is full of divine experiences these days, too numerous and private to share. I pray throughout the day and meditate weekly. When I give Reiki to people, I am not privy to their lives, problems, dreams, or hopes. I am truly on a "need to know basis." It has nothing to do with "me." I serve as a conduit, and there is no room for my ego. It is between my client and God. My Reiki experiences are like snowflakes: No two are alike, but all are incredibly beautiful. I pray to God and enlist His help for the divine highest good for all of us.

One afternoon I practiced my Reiki skills on Gib. He lay on his stomach on the massage table while an instrumental CD played. It was a relaxed environment, and I held my hand above his back feeling the energy flowing its warmth into his sore muscles. Then I felt an amazing burst of air push up against the palm of my hand. I stopped dead still and looked at that spot. I tried to process that sensation and just couldn't rationalize it. I finally lifted Gib's sweatshirt to peak underneath; did I expect to see something there that could push wind? It was crazy. Gib startled awake.

"Hey, what are you doing?" he asked.

"Sorry, Honey. I was just trying to figure something out."

"Huh. Well, Jesus was just here, and he had Gary with him."

Gary was the boy who shot Gib with a BB gun when they were young, and he died several years before as a result of an ATV accident: a very sad, tragic end to a young life. Gib continued with his story. "I haven't thought of Gary in years, Mom, but there he was looking wonderful and happy with Jesus. He said he was very sorry for hurting me like he did when we were kids. He said he only meant to scare me. I told him it was OK; I forgave him a long time ago. Then you woke me up before we could finishing talking," he stated.

"Gosh, that's wonderful Gib. I'm sorry to have interrupted that visit," I said. Then I thought of my experience. "By the way, where did he shoot you with that gun?"

Gib put his hand right on the spot where I had just felt the puff of air. "Right here," he said. I was stunned, absolutely incredulous.

It was a tough decision to include this story, because I felt Gary's family suffered enough pain in losing their son early in his life. If they were to read our story and see themselves in it, I would hate to remind them of that unpleasant business. Gib certainly forgave him and moved on, but the real importance of this story is the knowledge that healing continues on the other side of the veil as well. Gary was with Jesus; being healed, learning to forgive himself, presenting a gift for the rest of us to learn from. Not only does life continue after death, life continues to experience healing and forgiveness, as well. We are not dead in a stagnant state. We can continue to add value to the lives of others. The ugly incident became a joyful lesson to learn from.

Gib gave me that rosary Mary promised me for a Christmas gift. I giggle to remember how hard I worked at finding a "how to" guide. I wanted to learn the prayers and adapt them to my own needs. When I pray a "decade," which is a 10-bead section, I dedicate those prayers to a specific purpose or person. I intuited that Friday mornings would be my rosary time for God with my new best friend, Mary.

Gib continues to see Jesus, and I must admit I've caught His presence a few times, as well. He's there for anyone who invites him into his or her life, and when Gib and I pray together, we invite Jesus to join us. After all, the Bible records His promise to be wherever two or more are gathered in His name.

My meditations celebrate my gratitude. They are my one-on-one visits when I thank God for everything and include the grandiose as well as the minuscule. I appreciate the elements, the earth, the critters, the relationships, the universe, and all its inhabitants. I pray for all situations to be for our divine highest good.

Occasionally, we make it to church — not to find God so much as to fill our vessel full. The support is awesome, and I always hear something I needed to hear. If I didn't, I would find another church or keep looking until this need was filled. Life is too short to spend it with piety, bigotry, and falseness. It doesn't matter how we worship God, what methods or rituals we use. The only thing that matters is love and respect for Him and His family. Be in relationship with Him.

My insights continue to inspire me. One day, while exiting the shower — it doesn't get more humble than that — I heard this:

All people need to know is to invite Me into their lives. If your neighbor came to your door, he wouldn't enter without being asked in. Why would it be any different for Me?

It's that simple.

AFTERWORD

My wish for you, dear reader, is to find your connection to God. Learn to meditate. If you quiet the endless chatter and distractions from your mind, you will hear His whisper. Conquer your ego. If you consider yourself to be the master of your universe, you will never hear Him. Ask Him to share your life, your joys, and your sorrows. He will help you learn from them.

God is the life force for everything in this universe. His light is awesome. Every shadow disappears. Accept the miracles, or consequences, or grace — whatever you wish to call them — for the gifts that they are. As you embrace these gifts, your life will become so much more. But He is waiting to be invited in, so get going. The Creator has always loved you, so forgive yourself. Forgive others. Ask Him to share your life, protect you, guide you, and love you.

Ask, and you shall receive.

Hope is like a bird that senses the dawn and carefully starts to sing while it is still dark.
Anonymous